GROWING UP IN THE CHURCH

THIRD YEAR

Growing up in the Church

A Resource Book for
PRIMARY TEACHERS

THIRD YEAR

THE SAINT ANDREW PRESS
EDINBURGH

© THE SAINT ANDREW PRESS 1970
First Published in 1970
by the Saint Andrew Press
121 George Street, Edinburgh

ISBN 0 7152 0065 8

Reprinted August 1972

Printed by McCORQUODALE (Scotland) Ltd Glasgow

CONTENTS

Page

FOREWORD - - - - - - - - - - - - 7

A PROGRAMME OF CHRISTIAN EDUCATION - - - - 9

The Place of the Congregation - - - - - - - 11

Understanding the Primary Child - - - - - - 14

Communicating with the Primary Child - - - - - 18

Communicating through all kinds of Activities - - - - 22

Worship - - - - - - - - - - - 33

Preparing to Teach - - - - - - - - - 38

The Primary Teachers' Library - - - - - - - 42

Theme

1. BELONGING - - - - - - - - - - 43

2. THANKING GOD FOR THE WORLD HE HAS GIVEN US - 53

3. THE PEOPLE OF OUR CHURCH - - - - - - 64

4. CHRISTMAS - - - - - - - - - - 75

5. GOD'S WORLD IN WINTER - - - - - - - 88

6. CHOOSING - - - - - - - - - - 100

7. PRAISING AND THANKING GOD - - - - - - 110

8. EASTER - - - - - - - - - - 121

9. HELPING OTHERS - - - - - - - - - 135

10. A SUMMER THEME - - - - - - - - 147

HYMNS - - - - - - - - - - - 158

FOREWORD

In presenting to the Church this third volume of *Growing Up in the Church*, the Special Committee on Religious Education would once again express its most grateful thanks to the Baird and Russell Trusts, whose generous help has made publication possible.

The preparation of such a programme as this involves a number of people in a great deal of hard work. There is the planning and writing of the themes, their experimental use in a number of Sunday schools; and the subsequent panelling, revising and final drafting of the whole for the printer. In this volume, most of this work, both on the themes and the introduction, has been done by Mrs. Cynthia Dean, aided by her husband, the Rev. John Dean. To them both, the committee owes a debt of gratitude.

We take this opportunity of thanking all the other writers who have contributed to this volume: Mrs. Bolton to Theme 1, Rev. J. McDonald to Theme 2, Miss Morrison to Theme 5, Mrs. Mather and Mrs. Cameron to Theme 10 and Miss J. Low to the Needs of the Primary Child, and also all the teachers, leaders and children, in the experimental centres, for their helpful criticism and suggestion.

Thanks are also due to the Rev. Dr. John Gray, Miss G. Fleming and Miss Joan Low, whose advice and help on the reading panel were of the greatest value. The Rev. J. I. H. McDonald, and his successor as Baird Fellow, the Rev. V. C. Pogue, together with the Rev. Ian M. Fairweather, have given invaluable help, the last contributing to the introduction.

To Miss Jean Notman, secretary to the Baird Fellow and the Special Committee, is due a special word of thanks. Her work for this volume, and for the whole programme, has been far in excess of the many duties laid upon her.

Finally, mention should be made of the help and advice, always available, from the Rev. G. B. Hewitt, Secretary of the Department of Education, the Rev. Dr. A. W. Sawyer, Convener of the Special Committee on Religious Education, and from Messrs. T. B. Honeyman and J. S. Geekie of the Saint Andrew Press.

It will be seen that this has been a co-operative effort and, as such, it is presented to the Church in the hope that it may be a useful instrument in the Christian nurture of those for whom it is intended.

Introduction

A PROGRAMME OF CHRISTIAN EDUCATION

This third volume of *Growing Up in the Church* completes the three-year cycle of material for the Primary stage of a programme of Christian education extending from Baptism to First Communion. The Primary department is concerned with children of five to seven years inclusive, as they are growing up within the Christian community. The volumes are intended for use in turn during a period of three years, the whole department dealing with the same volume and the same theme at the same time. Because children are developing during their three years in the Primary, each volume contains material for both older and younger children.

It is called a Programme of Christian Education because far more is being offered than suggestions for lesson material which teachers can accept or reject at will. There are certain basic principles on which the programme is built without which it cannot be implemented; but there is ample scope for adapting the programme to meet local needs without changing these basic principles.

Christian education is said to be: *Church Based, Gospel Centred,* and *Child Related.*

The task of Christian education is *Christian Nurture,* for which the Church is the agent as she responds to the Gospel in her worship, witness and obedience. The Church in which the child is being nurtured is the people of God both in the world, and in the local congregation. The child meets the Church first in his own home, the Christian family, and then in the local congregation which is the family of God. He grows up in the Church in both these ways.

CHURCH BASED

Christian education is a continuing process. Our nurture in the Church never ceases. There is no point at which we can say that we "stand complete" and need no further enlightening. We are all growing in grace towards Christian maturity. There is an informal, or unconscious, process of education going on all the time, for adults as well as for children, as the Church responds to the Gospel. In this total task the Sunday school is charged with carrying out a programme of Christian education.

The Gospel of God's love is central in the life of the Church and in Christian nurture. It is to this love the child must respond if he is to grow up as a child of God. The young child responds not to words that speak about the Gospel, but to the love that embodies and expresses the Gospel. The parent, or leader, who shows love, care, acceptance, and understanding to the child is conveying God's love to him and communicating the Gospel in the only possible and vital way for the child—through his experience (cf. 1 John 4: 7-8).

GOSPEL CENTRED

It is essential for the teacher always to think in terms of the child learning rather than of the teacher teaching. The child learns all the time, and not just at those times when we think we are teaching him.

9

A*

**CHILD
RELATED**

The teacher must try to enter the world of the child. She will only be able to do this by observing the child's behaviour, and not by trying to remember her own childhood. Childhood memories are overlaid by adult interpretations. The teacher must make a deliberate effort to separate her observation of what she actually sees and hears from possible interpretations of the behaviour. Unless she can learn to do this, she will never be able to enter the world of the child.

The child learns through his senses and his experiences. He learns as the teacher talks with him not only in the informal talks, but as he engages in activities. It is to enable the child to learn in the most appropriate way for him that so much stress is laid on activities in the programme, and that the provision of a choice of activities is essential.

In all our teaching we must start where the child is, with his experience, or with experience that will be meaningful for him, that is experience that he can recognise as similar to his own. We must also proceed from the known to the unknown, since it is our aim to deepen and extend the experience. We must begin with his present experience and build on that. A teacher, in informal talks, may find it difficult to find a suitable place to begin ; but a good knowledge of the individual children will help her to do so.

Children are not yet ready for the teacher to describe in words something beyond the range of their experience ; nor are they yet able to put into words what they have learnt. They are much more at home in engaging with the theme through activities of various kinds. In the Primary, the teacher does not need to be restricted to talks. When the children begin the activities there will be moments when, as she talks with the children while they are engaged in the activity of their choice, learning will go on more effectively because it is related to what they are doing. The teacher must continually try to provide an environment in which the children will experience love and so respond to the Gospel of the Grace and Love of God in appropriate ways.

WORSHIP

If the process of Christian nurture is to be complete children and young people must be introduced to, and participate in, the Church's public worship. They also need to worship in ways appropriate to their age and stage of development.

This programme incorporates these two distinct aspects of worship, the worship of the Christian family in the local congregation, that is the adult service in church, and also worship in ways suitable to the children's age and stage of development in the Primary room. Worship is dealt with at length in another section of the introduction (see p. 33).

THE PLACE OF THE CONGREGATION IN CHRISTIAN EDUCATION

The whole Church, as the People of God, not the Sunday school alone, is involved in Christian education. Christian education is a continuous process which takes place all the time and not just at chosen periods when the child is in the Primary room.

The congregation, by all that it does in response or otherwise to the Gospel, is transmitting attitudes and values which have lasting effects upon the young. If, for example, the worship of the church, when the children are present, is dull and uninteresting, they are being given a wrong idea of worship. Again, if the church hall is clean, well looked after and the atmosphere bright and welcoming, they get the impression that the congregation is concerned about them, and is glad to see them. Children are sensitive to atmosphere and they notice and imitate attitudes.

It is necessary, therefore, for the congregation to be made aware of the role it plays in Christian education, becoming more involved in the work of the Sunday school, understanding its aims, and doing what it can to help.

Christian Education Group

To give focus to the Church's teaching ministry it is essential to establish at the outset a Christian Education Group, on the lines suggested in previous publications. It should include the minister, representatives of the Kirk Session and other office-bearers (e.g. deacons, managers, members of the congregational board), Sunday school leaders, parents' representatives, Woman's Guild and Young Wives' and Mothers' Group representatives, and any others the local situation might deem advisable.

The task of the group would be:
   (i) To study and understand the meaning of Christian education in the Church, and in particular the aims and implications of the new programme;
   (ii) To find ways and means of providing the facilities required for the Christian education programme in the Church;
   (iii) To facilitate the introduction and operation of the whole Christian education programme at successive stages of the Sunday school;
   (iv) To help to interest and involve parents and congregation in the Christian education of the young people, and thereby incidentally to promote adult education;
   (v) To co-operate with the Session in encouraging all children of Church families to attend Sunday school, and to consider what practical steps should be taken to reach children in the parish not receiving any Christian education.

This Christian Education Group, which is representative of the main agencies in the congregation, will forge links with young parents, the Young Wives' and Mothers' Group, the Woman's Guild and the Men's Club. It will seek ways of making these groups aware of their role as members of the congregation in Christian nurture, and encourage them to work in practical ways to facilitate the introduction and operation of the whole Christian education programme.

The formation of a Christian Education Group should provide an impetus to Church life not only through the education given to the young, but should also create a sense of community within the congregation.

A sense of community

There is a need in Christian nurture for the children to become aware of the Church as a community, larger and more comprehensive than their own family. The Church is much more than a collection of individuals, and each congregation must seek ways of making more real the fact that it is a family of those who care for one another. It is within this community that children find the care and love which are derived from the Gospel, and discover that the church consists of real people who worship and serve God, not only on Sunday but in their everyday lives. On several occasions in the themes in this volume, the children are given the opportunity to meet some of the people of the church. In Theme 3, "The People of Our Church," the children are encouraged to talk about the people they know, who come to their church, and it is suggested that people such as the church officer, the flower convener, the church treasurer and an elder meet and talk with the children in the Primary room. In Theme 5, a joiner or handyman may help the children to erect a bird-table in the church grounds, and in Theme 7, a mother, shopkeeper, and other suitable people may be asked to talk about their work. Whenever people are to help in this way, they should be invited to attend the preparation class so that they may understand what is expected of them and why. In this way members of the congregation will get an insight into the aims of Christian nurture by becoming involved in some part of the programme.

Contact with the homes of the children

Parents have a vital role to play in the Christian nurture of their children. It is therefore essential that contact is made and maintained with them, to interest them in what the Primary is doing and also in the Christian education programme as a whole. They need to understand how children grow up in the Church, learn and develop towards maturity in Christ and how what is done in the Primary and at other stages helps that growth and development.

WORKSHEETS

A useful link with the home is the worksheet, with an explanation of the theme in the footnote for parents. At the end of each theme, whether the child has completed the worksheet or not, he can take it home to show to his parents. To enable parents and members of the congregation to know in advance the theme being attempted in the Primary, a brief outline of it might be printed in the church magazine.

Parents may be encouraged to visit the Primary from time to time, provided their presence does not disrupt the normal procedure. Time might also be set aside for a Parents' Evening when they can be shown some of the work done by the children.

VISITATION

Visiting the homes of the children by teachers supplements the contacts made by the Christian Education Group, and shows the concern of the congregation for the children in its care. To see a child in his own home, or to see a child's home even though he is not there at the time, helps the teacher to understand him better.

To be effective, visitation should be done regularly, not only when a child is absent, for he may then think that he is being "got at" through his parents to attend. Teachers are often shy about calling upon people they do not know well. They do not know if they will be welcome, or if they may be intruding when the family is looking at TV, or entertaining friends. Before making a first visit, it would be advisable for the teacher to consult the district elder. Teachers will discover that in most cases a short visit is appreciated, and once contact is made, visiting will become pleasant and rewarding.

The regular visitation of the homes of the children should be regarded as something quite different from visiting the children when they are ill, or have been absent from the Primary for a prolonged period.

Sick visiting

Visiting a child with serious or prolonged illness, whether in hospital or at home, should not be overlooked. The leader, or teacher, should visit the home, and if she informs the minister, he will also visit the child and his family. Sometimes, as with the practical project suggested in Theme 9, "Helping Others," p. 135, the Primary children themselves can be engaged in making a present or a card to send to a sick child.

Prolonged absence

A child with prolonged absence from the Primary, for reasons other than sickness, requires a visit from the leader or teacher. The visit should be paid in a friendly and helpful spirit, to discover why the child has not attended (without being too inquisitive), and to show the continuing interest of the Church in the child. In these instances, too, the minister should be informed.

YOUTH ROLL

The names of the children in the Primary should be on the "Youth Roll," which contains the names of all baptised children and others in all the organisations of the church. These names should remain on the Youth Roll until the young people become communicant members of the Church. If a child's name is dropped from the roll of the Primary at the beginning of a session because of prolonged absence in the previous session and his non-appearance in the first few weeks of the new one, even after a visit from the leader or teacher, then the Youth Roll will ensure that his name is not dropped from the care of the congregation. This roll might be divided into districts like the Communion Roll, each elder being concerned for both adults and children in the homes of his district.

UNDERSTANDING THE PRIMARY CHILD

Each child is
different

Every child is an individual, a unique person with his own potentialities and limitations, growing and developing at his own rate. Getting to know and understand each child as an individual and learning to respect him as a person in his own right is necessary if the teacher is going to help him to "grow in grace and knowledge" towards Christian maturity. Christian education is concerned with the development of the child as a person, involving his whole life and not just a small facet of his personality.

NEEDS OF THE PRIMARY CHILD

Although each child is different, there are certain basic needs and characteristics that are common to most and the child is dependent on the adult to meet these needs. Every child needs to be loved and to respond to love, to feel accepted and secure, and to feel a sense of belonging.

Love

The need to be loved is an essential part of all human nature; this is how we are made. The yearning for love is God given; and should lead finally into relationship with God, which is the fulfilment of his purpose in making man (John 17: 3). It is through parents and others that the love of God is first brought to the child, enabling his spirit to grow. If these "channels" are blocked, damage is done which may be permanent.

If the child is to develop fully, he needs this kind of love, the love that God mediates through parents and teacher, and through the Christian congregation. It is to this love that the child responds. No matter how withdrawn the child is, the teacher must try to remain warm and friendly and not to force the child to talk or to join in any activity. Sometimes the child will be very independent and want to do everything for himself; he should be encouraged to do so. At other times the same child will want to be helped, comforted, even babied. A sensitive teacher will be aware of this and will respond to the need of the child. Support and encouragement are often necessary, but sometimes the child should be allowed to get on with what he has to do without interference from adults.

He must not be rejected because he is disobedient, restless or difficult, but must find that in all circumstances he is cared for by his teacher and that she is concerned for his well-being. If he is genuinely loved he will be accepted unreservedly and forgiven when need arises.

Acceptance

A child knows that he is accepted when what he has drawn or painted or written is appreciated by his teacher, who does not expect adult skills but values children's work. When spelling is odd, or the model he had made from scrap materials is weird, the teacher still delights in what he has done. Teachers must accept that it is quite normal that some may be able to read and some may not, that some can write stories, and that some have neither the ability nor the desire to do so.

A sense of
belonging

Within the church the child should feel that he belongs. Here he will find happy relationships not only with his teacher and the children with whom he plays or who co-operate with him in some activity, but also with the minister and members of the congregation. Adults are willing to talk with him, listen to him, show him where things are to be found and always to be helpful. This is the family of God to which he belongs and he is gladly accepted in it. Parents, teachers and adults in the congregation may fail to make a good relationship with a particular child but they will know that the failure is in themselves, not in the child. Maturity is not to be expected in children, but Christian maturity should enable adults to accept them as they are.

Security

A child needs to feel secure and such security is given by a teacher who shows herself to be dependable, consistent in her reactions, friendly and unruffled in her attitudes. Through her interest in the child, she builds up a sense of trust which is essential for a good relationship.

Such a sense of security helps the child to adapt himself to changing situations, to grow without fear mentally and socially, to express his own ideas and to experiment with materials and in social relationships. When he is secure he is more willing to share, to give way, or take turns; to develop initiative and independence and to use his imagination and reasoning powers.

Children are more secure when they know what is expected of them. There are simple rules which must be maintained. There is a limit to what the teacher will allow, because her concern for each child includes their respect for others.

CHARACTERISTICS OF THE PRIMARY CHILD

Always active

The normal healthy Primary child is full of energy and is almost ceaselessly active. He can't sit still for very long. He loves to be moving about doing things. He listens, asks, touches, looks, tastes and smells, in fact, he uses all his senses to discover and to understand the world around him and he should have the opportunity to explore in this way if he is to develop as a person and grow towards maturity. The more first-hand sensory experiences he encounters at this stage, the richer his future thinking will be.

Wants to learn

The Primary child wants to learn, he is curious and asks many questions. He wants to know why? what for? where? how? and requires short, definite answers. He lives in and for the present. Time, for him, is today, Christmas, my birthday, when the summer comes. He is impulsive and wilful, his self-control is not fully developed, and his vocabulary and experiences are limited. He imitates, imagines and is highly suggestible, his span of attention is brief and his interests often short-lived. "This is how the Primary child describes himself through his behaviour and feelings as well as his words:[1]

"I like to be active;
I can't sit still long;
I am not co-ordinated;
my muscles aren't strong.
I'm proud of my family,
I'm eager to learn.
My world is expanding,
for experiences I yearn.

I'm creative, imaginative;
I draw what I think.
I sense adults' moods
and their good attitudes.
I like to do important things
such as flying away
on butterfly wings!"

[1] "The Way of Love," Helen Munson—*United Church Press.*

Imitates

The Primary child imitates and copies what he sees in the adult world. He plays at mummies and daddies, schools, hospitals, shops, reflecting adult actions and tones of voice. He learns through participating in informal drama and in such situations he can play out some of his fears and difficulties; problems which he cannot put into words. In his play he learns about the world in which he lives, himself and other people.

Imagines

The imaginary world is very real to the child. Alan, apparently charging round the room, is found to be riding his camel. The child, running with a stick, waving his hand, may be flying the latest jet aircraft. He does not easily distinguish between fantasy and reality. He can take part unselfconsciously in drama without elaborate props, e.g., a large cardboard carton quickly becomes a train or a boat, and he can enter sympathetically into some of the experiences of others. As he grows, his imagination becomes more controlled and his ability to concentrate increases.

Goes to school

During his stay in the Primary, the child's world is widening and his interests turn freely to things and people outside his own home. He now goes to school and this contributes largely to the broadening of his horizons. In school he is being helped to develop new skills and much of his learning is in informal ways suited to his own interests. Though the Sunday school is not a copy of the day school, teachers must recognise that a child's needs and the way he learns are the same whether it is Sunday or Monday.

Develops skills

At five years of age the firmer muscles of the hand are not fully co-ordinated and it is difficult for the child to do things that require great control. He needs large thick crayons and large pieces of blank paper for drawings (not a post-card and pencil). As he grows, his skills will develop and, since children are all different, it is difficult to generalise about what they are capable of doing at certain ages. It is for this reason that the teacher must think not simply about the group but about the individual children in it.

**Free
to choose**

The child's freedom to choose the kind of activity he engages in should be respected. Not only does this ensure his interest is in what he is doing, but it also encourages growth towards independence, self-direction and self-discipline. If the child does not want to learn in the way that the teacher wants then some other means must be sought, because he learns best when he willingly participates.

Participates in learning

The child must be involved in what is being done because only then will learning be effective. By sharing an experience the child knows about something, not just because he has been told, but because the experience has become part of him. The more varied and meaningful his experience is, and the more actively he takes part in it, the more likely it is that learning will take place.

Develops at his own pace

In the development of a child there are various stages, and every child must pass through these stages at his own pace. Some progress rapidly, others more slowly but steadily. Learning starts at birth, and the child learns much in the first five years. He learns from his environment by observation and by active participation and experiment. The child then has a background of experience on which the teacher can build.

The teacher should begin with a familiar experience, something the child understands or is already interested in. From this the unknown is explored, leading the child to a new experience. When children are interested in anything they are keen to discover more about it. Adults can stimulate their interest, answer their questions, make suggestions and direct their enthusiasm, in no way dominating, but giving the chance to explore.

Learns through experience

Communication involves giving and receiving, action and response. The teacher may use stories, music, drama and creative activities to enable the child to receive some understanding of life and experience and encourage him to express what he is learning through paint, clay, music and language.

The child learns most through his relationships with others, children of his own age, and adults. His relationship with his teacher is important. In a quiet, unobtrusive manner she can provide an atmosphere in which he feels able to be himself amongst friends.

Learns through relationships

GETTING TO KNOW THE CHILDREN

It is important that the teacher should know each child in her group. If she is to do this she must watch them at play and at work, talk with them informally and, most important, listen to what they say to each other and to other adults. She should try to catch the meaning of what they say as well as the words. She must listen to what they tell her, even when it has nothing to do with Sunday school. She needs to see the things they do, what they choose and how they plan and work together. She must show them how interested she is in them, talk with them and answer their questions. Only they can show what is interesting and important to them. Only they can show what they are ready to understand, what their difficulties are and what is the range of their present knowledge, what can satisfy them and where they need help. Whenever she can, the teacher should ask, "What do you think? What are your ideas? Where did you find that out?" She should not do all the talking, or make all the suggestions, or she will miss what is most important, the child's own thoughts and ideas.

Listen

Observe

Ask questions

COMMUNICATING WITH THE PRIMARY CHILD

THE THEMES

The ten themes, which give cohesion to this programme, present the Gospel to the child in the context of his own living and experience and are designed to help him at his present stage of development to respond to God in his daily life.

Young children are not able to reason from one logical step to another, nor are they able to follow an adult train of thought, but as they actively work at the themes in conversation and stories and engage in the various activities, they explore vital areas of their experience. They learn how to live and are helped in the most fundamental type of learning.

Related to experience

Teaching must begin with, and relate to, the child's own first-hand experience, but experience should not be confused with interest, it is much more than this. What the child feels and understands, what becomes part of his inmost being, part of himself—is experience. But teaching must also attempt to widen and deepen his present experience without going beyond his understanding. For example, in the harvest theme (p. 53), the teacher begins by talking with the children about the kind of heating they use at home, the one that is most familiar to them, she then attempts to deepen their experience by introducing a story about another form of heating. She talks with them about the harvest festival in their own church and then, by means of a story, introduces them to a harvest service in Santalia.

Biblical material

All the themes are biblically based and teachers should study the biblical foundations in detail at the preparation class before the theme goes into operation.

Biblical material which illumines the experience of the children is the focal point of all the themes. The themes deal with the kind of experiences the children can easily recognise in their own everyday life; experiences of loving, thanking, sharing, helping and caring for others and only in this way does the content of the Bible become meaningful to them.

Caring is central in the life of Jesus and is expressed by the Christian community in kindness, helpfulness, friendliness and compassion, that is, in action for the sake of others. Christianity means to feed the hungry, clothe the naked, help the sick (Matt. 25: 31-46). As Primary children share in the church's ministry of caring for others they see that they are part of the worshipping community who show their love for God as they love and serve their fellow men.

THE GROUPS

Each teacher in the Primary should be directly responsible for a group of about eight children. In large Primaries, the group may have to be larger than this and in this case it is advisable for the teacher to have an assistant who is learning to be a teacher. Where there are so many children in the group that the teacher cannot really know each child, the group is too large. It takes a long time to *know* each child but if the teacher is in charge of the same group for a whole session she can really get to know them.

She keeps a record of attendance, enquires about absentees and visits the homes of children who are ill or have not attended for a few weeks. Children enjoy receiving a card or letter from their teacher and friends when they are absent; it assures them that they have been missed and that there is a welcome for them when they return. A card could be made and sent by the group when anyone is ill or absent for more than two Sundays.

The teacher should establish and maintain regular contact with the parents. Where teachers have established a good relationship with the children and their parents, they have found that the informal talks, particularly those concerning homes and families, have been much easier to lead. In the class groups the children are happy to share their news with their teacher and their friends. Sometimes this leads quite naturally into the informal talk or story but at other times the teacher has to take the initiative and turn their attention to the theme which she introduces in her own way. The story or talk should *not* be introduced by the leader from the front, except in very small Primaries with less than a dozen children or when a filmstrip is used.

At the beginning of a new session the teacher should learn the names of the children in her own group as quickly as possible. It is helpful if every child is given a badge with his name printed clearly on it, then as the children move from their class groups to the activities the leader and other teachers also learn their names. The leader and teachers should also wear a badge so that the children learn their names, too. It is important for the child to be identified immediately by his name, rather than to be referred to as "you," or, "the boy in the blue jersey." He feels that he belongs if, for instance, the teacher in charge of the painting group can say, "*Ian*, will you please fetch some clean water for the painting?" rather than, "What's your name? I know you told me last week, but I've forgotten it again." To every child his name is very important.

Names

Each class might be given its own particular colour of badge or, alternatively, two colours might be used to distinguish the older and younger sections. Badges can be bought, but if the teacher makes her own she can make them much larger and of a type the children can manage to put on and take off themselves.

THE INFORMAL TALK

The informal talk is an important means of communicating with the Primary child. It is a conversation between the teacher and the children in her group; it is not a lesson, with the teacher talking to the children while they listen, but rather a sharing of interests and experiences. In discussion, the children make their own contribution, and learning takes place.

The outlines of the talks in the programme are intended only as guides for the teacher as she prepares. They are suggestions for a discussion to which she encourages the children to contribute. If the teacher is familiar with the topic and has a clear grasp of the aim of the talk there should be a lively interchange of ideas between the teacher and her group.

This kind of approach requires experience and practice but as the teacher acquires this skill she will learn how to develop the outline in her own way to suit the needs of her own particular group. She will also learn to make the transition from the informal chatting and sharing of news, as the children gather in their groups, to the theme for the day. For example, Janet was showing the new dress, that her granny had made, to her group. The subject of the informal talk was "Using our hands" and so the teacher was able to say, "Janet's granny used material, scissors, a needle and cotton and a sewing machine to make this lovely new dress, but what else did she use? Yes, she used her hands." This led the children on to discuss all the things they can do and make with their hands.

Very often there is one child in the group who tries to dominate the conversation and it may be necessary for the teacher to direct questions to other members of the group so that all the children get a chance to contribute.

A few children are shy and retiring and do not join in the discussion easily. Only the teacher who knows the child well will know just how far she can draw this child into the conversation. Teachers who are new to this approach, those who are training to be teachers and those whose children either do not talk very readily or chatter among themselves too much, often require a picture or an object to help the group to turn their attention to the theme. Posters, games to play and books containing suitable pictures for introducing the discussion are suggested throughout this volume. The teacher should look ahead through the themes and collect, from magazines and catalogues, suitable photographs and pictures of food, clothing, birds, people at work, families, etc., which she can then mount to make a poster or book ready to introduce the talks.

One teacher was encouraging her group to talk about the things they see and do in the church when John, aged five, commented that the photograph of the Communion table which she showed looked like a party. The teacher very wisely used his contribution to tell the group that the Communion service is "like a party," it is a time when all the people of the church meet together to share a meal. The teacher was using this familiar experience, something the children understood and were already interested in, to lead them to a new experience.

Talking informally with the group takes time if teacher and children are to listen to each other and therefore it cannot be hurried. In the informal talk, as ideas are shared and new insights reached, the teacher has the opportunity to know what the children are thinking, to discover their interests and needs and to lead them to new experiences essential for their growth.

THE STORY

Most children love stories and are usually ready to listen to them, provided they are told, or read, well. It takes practice to become a good storyteller and the teacher must always prepare carefully if she is going to tell the story without hesitation.

A story usually follows a pattern or framework and is a unit in itself. A good beginning captures the children's interest and attention, the main characters are introduced and the action develops; the climax points indirectly to the aim in telling that particular story and the conclusion is brief.

The teacher's chair should be low enough for easy contact with her listeners and she and the children should be sitting comfortably and feel ready to enjoy the story. The story should be told vividly and naturally in words that all the children understand. Conversation between characters and even a different tone of voice for some of them helps to make the story more interesting. If the teacher looks at the children as she tells the story, they will listen more readily than if she looks at her book. When the teacher is familiar with the story and enjoys telling it, then it comes alive and the children become absorbed in the narrative. They identify themselves with the characters, participate in the action and enter fully into the situation.

Some of the stories are written so that the teacher can stop at certain points to allow the children to add their own comments, discuss an interesting point, or ask a question.

The stories are short and are not intended to be expanded by the teacher unless the points raised or questions asked by the children demand it. The teacher should guard against using "religious" language, adding a "moral" or "talking down" to the children.

Choosing to read the story, rather than telling it, is not an easy way out for the teacher, for it needs as much careful preparation. If the teacher is to hold the attention of her group she must be thoroughly familiar with the story, practising it several times beforehand if her reading of it is to be of a high enough standard to sustain the children's attention.

Only a few stories are repeated in the whole of the three-year Primary cycle, but children love repetition and learn by hearing stories more than once.

A short, well-told story can be repeated if the children request it, or it can be enjoyed as an activity in the Book Corner.

Stories about Jesus have been selected carefully to show the Gospel in action in ways the child can understand.

THE FILMSTRIP

The informal talk and story, speaking and listening are the means of communicating verbally with Primary children but a filmstrip or set of slides used with skill, imagination, and discretion provide an effective way of visual communication. The filmstrip which is relevant to the theme and suitable for Primary children should be obtained well in advance and viewed by the teachers at the preparation class before it is presented to the children. In this volume, the third and fourth parts of the filmstrip "People Show God's Love" are used in Theme 2 and the first and second parts of "This Wonderful World" in Theme 10.

It is essential to have the necessary equipment set up and tried out before the session begins. There is nothing more distracting than to have people fixing plugs, uncoiling wire and threading the filmstrip as the children arrive. It is often easier to blackout a small, well-ventilated room than the larger Primary room but after seeing the filmstrip the children should return to their own room to work at the activities.

Skill is required to put the filmstrip in correctly and operate the projector efficiently and, if there is not a skilled projectionist in the department, a member of the congregation may be invited to assist.

For Primary children, ten or twelve frames are sufficient for one showing and although the leader is familiar with the commentary she should not be tied to it but should involve the children through questions and conversation. Where the filmstrip captures the interest of the children, this interest may be extended ; for instance, after seeing part two of "People Show God's Love," the children in one Primary were shown round the local dairy by one of the elders who worked there.

If a projector is not available for showing the filmstrip, the written commentary published in this volume provides an excellent outline for a story.

COMMUNICATING THROUGH ALL KINDS OF ACTIVITIES

An integral part of the programme

The activities, which should occupy the longest stretch of time in the Primary, are not just an optional extra to keep the children's interest, or to fill in time ; they are a necessary part of the programme every week and provide a situation in which the children become involved in their own learning. As the children participate in the activities they continue to learn about the theme, expressing their ideas and feelings in an imaginative and creative way ; discussing and sharing, working and co-operating with other children and with their teachers in a relaxed and industrious atmosphere. Working with all kinds of creative materials gives the children an opportunity to think, reason, plan, imagine, experiment, explore, discover, invent and create, all important aspects essential to their development.

A choice of activities

The Primary room must be set out by the teachers with a variety of activities before the session begins. A rota of teachers might be established so that only one or two need to arrive early each week to prepare the room. If some of the basic materials for painting, crayoning, model-making, dramatisation and worksheets are set out in the same area of the room each week, the children become familiar with the layout and know where to find the activity of their choice.

Every week when new activities, such as making puppets, collage pictures or posters are introduced they should be pointed out to the children, either by the leader or the group teacher. After the story or talk, the teacher should discuss, with the children in her group, the activities that are available before they choose.

To guide Primary staffs as they prepare, a summary of the main activities is given below. For further information the teachers should read the appropriate notes in *Growing Up in the Church—First and Second Years.*

PAINTING: materials required

For painting, the children require a variety of large brushes with long handles, jars or yogurt cartons for water, aprons to protect their clothes, assorted colours, shapes and sizes of paper and a choice of the type of paint they use (e.g., powder colour mixed to a thick creamy consistency and paint in solid form—"*Opake*" *colour cakes*), provided in six or eight colours: vermilion, cobalt, mid-chrome, crimson, viridian, burnt umber, black and white, from which other colours can be mixed. Small amounts of powder colour, one part powder to four parts water, prepared frequently, help to keep the colours bright and attractive and is more economical in use. The material should be arranged either on low tables or on the floor. The tables and floor can be protected with newspaper or plastic sheets.

Individual paintings

Large quantities of drawing-paper, sugar paper or wallpaper (size 18" x 14") are required for individual paintings, as most children in the younger groups are not yet ready to work on a group painting. They often enjoy experimenting with colours, putting paint on to paper without knowing what they are painting. This the teacher must encourage, since it is a stage through which they must grow before they begin to paint what they intend. At this stage, the teacher should talk about painting rather than painting a "picture" and she should not expect the child to say what his painting *is* every time he paints, but should share his delight in his achievement. Children enjoy making large free paintings and the teacher should resist giving them outlines, or showing them how to paint, as this destroys their creativity.

A group frieze

Later, usually at the age of six or seven years, depending on his experience of paint and of his environment, the child wants to give his painting a title and is ready to work with other children on a group frieze. Rolls of wallpaper or shelf paper can be used by a group of children to make a frieze which is an excellent means of portraying a story or theme visually. If the teacher discusses the subject of the frieze with the children before they begin to paint, the pictures will then be richer and fuller as the ideas are incorporated in the frieze.

Care of materials

By careful planning, the amount of mess the children make with paints can be reduced. The teacher in charge of the painting activity should provide a brush for each container of liquid paint and remind the children to wipe the brush on the side of the container to prevent drips. For children using solid paints, two inches of water in a container is quite sufficient if changed frequently and avoids the mess made by a jam jar full of dirty water if an accident occurs. Jars of liquid paint can be stored in a large shoe or biscuit box and the solid paints, usually obtained in stacking palettes, can be stored easily after the paint has dried. Brushes must be treated with respect and the children should be taught how to use them carefully. They should not be left lying around, stiff with paint, but must be washed properly and dried well, after use. They should always be stored in an upright position and should *never* be left standing on their bristles. A good supply of rags or paper towels is essential.

COLLAGE

A collage picture is made of scraps of material of various colours, shapes and textures glued on to a background of strong paper or cardboard. The children may draw their own outlines with a wax crayon but there is no need for them to draw on the pieces of material as the shapes and colours provided by the teacher usually suggest the picture.

A collage picture made by the younger children may not resemble any specific thing at first. They need time to experiment with the materials and to enjoy creating a picture with the various shapes and textures. A flannelgraph board and a box of scraps of material which adhere to it without using glue might be used as an introduction to collage. As they become more skilled in the use of collage materials a group of children might work together to make a frieze.

Obviously, if the children are making a life-size collage picture, the scraps of material they use must also be large. For smaller pictures, smaller scraps of material are required as children do find difficulty in cutting small bits from a large piece of material even when they are using good scissors.

Suitable materials

Buttons, beads, feathers, cotton, nylon, wool, lace, silk, velvet, wallpaper, metallic foil paper and seeds of various shapes and sizes can be collected by the teachers and the children. Coloured pieces of advertisements cut from magazines and catalogues provide an excellent range of colours for collage. Odd scraps of sheep's wool, rug wool, nylon stockings, string and raffia are useful for the hair of people the children put into their pictures. An autumn picture might include coloured leaves, seed heads and cones. The children need small scissors (4½″ size) sharp enough to cut the material and the teacher should have a large pair available in case they are required. A selection of different kinds of adhesive should also be available. The "polycel" type will stick the thin materials, but "Gloy Multiglue," "Bostic," or "UHU" is required for buttons, feathers and seeds. At first the children may need help and guidance from the teacher about which adhesive to use with which material. The children should be shown how to cut with the scissors and use the glue.

After painting or drawing, the children can cut out the figures and shapes and group them together to make a group frieze by glueing the pieces on to a coloured background.

Sometimes the teacher may have to prepare the background beforehand owing to the shortage of time in the Sunday session, but usually it is sufficient to glue together a piece of blue paper for the sea and yellow paper for the sand to make a background for a seaside theme. (Theme 10.)

MODEL-MAKING materials

The shapes and sizes of cartons and scrap material suggest a model to the children more readily than a sheet of flat modelling cardboard.

Shoe boxes, lollipop sticks, "Vim" tins, cheese boxes, egg boxes, match-boxes, corrugated cardboard, pipe-cleaners, a variety of cartons, scraps of fabric, sheep's wool, rug wool, string, toilet roll tubes, will all be useful and can be stored in a large cardboard carton.

Scissors that cut, various kinds of strong glue, e.g., "Gloy Multiglue" and "Copydex," strong gummed paper, brass-headed paper fasteners and a stapler are also necessary for model-making.

Making figures

Figures of people and animals can be made from clothes-pegs, newspaper rolls, the children's own drawings and all kinds of scrap materials. (See *Growing Up in the Church, First Year*, pp. 26-28 ; and *Second Year*, pp. 22-23, for diagrams and instructions.) Throughout this volume, in the appropriate themes, suggestions are given for making various kinds of figures.

Pliable modelling materials, "Plasticine," "Aloplast," "Play-doh," salt and flour dough, and clay should also be available on another table for the children to use.

When the making of a model is being introduced, the teacher should sit with the group of children and discuss with them the possibilities of the materials and be with them to give help and advice when it is required. The success of a model depends largely on the choice and quality of the materials provided and the way the teacher introduces it to them. Making a model takes time and will probably require more than one week. Children are often enthusiastic the first week, not a bit interested the next, but return to complete the work later. Teachers must not always expect finished results, as the children need to discover the possibilities of the materials they are using. They also need to play with the models they have made and learning about the theme continues as they do so.

DRAWING and CRAYONING

The children should be encouraged to use their imagination as they make their large free drawings, and teachers should not provide outlines for them. They need thick wax crayons and felt pens in a variety of bright colours and various shapes and sizes of fairly thick paper. (Newsprint is too thin for drawing and crayoning.)

The children should be encouraged to experiment with the crayons rather than producing only line drawings with them. A variety of effects can be obtained with wax crayons depending upon the pressure put on them, the way they are held and the type of surface the paper has.

WRITING

Many children enjoy writing "stories." Sometimes a child will ask the teacher to write a story under his drawing or painting, e.g., "This is my tractor." Some children write at considerable length. No attempt should be made to correct a child's effort, even if it seems completely incomprehensible ! If a child asks how to write or spell a word the teacher should write it on a piece of paper for him. This is better than spelling it out as the child may not know the letters by name, only by sound. Most children are accustomed to writing on blank paper so there should be an ample supply of such paper of various sizes, shapes and, if possible, colours and a variety of thick, soft lead pencils and crayons.

In areas where I.T.A. (Initial Teaching Alphabet) is taught in day schools the children are eager to show the Primary teacher how they write. Children using this method are usually

When a Samaritan traveller came along he went to the man and bathed his wounds.

quite eager to help each other with the spelling and write fluently and creatively. The Primary teacher must not embarrass or inhibit the child by making fun of his attempts but should give him encouragement to write. The teacher will find that she can read this writing quite easily.

Scrapbooks

The drawings, crayoning and writing done by the children can be used in many different ways. Most children enjoy seeing their work displayed. They can help the teachers to glue the work they have done into a scrapbook, or on to a poster or a TV strip. (See *Growing Up in the Church, First Year,* p. 58, and *Second Year,* p. 24.)

Posters

TV Strip

If all the children who choose this activity portray the same part of the story then obviously a poster has to be made of *all* their drawings, but if the teacher discusses the story with the children before they begin and explains the scrapbook or TV strip to them, they usually volunteer to illustrate different parts of the story.

DRAMATISATION

Materials useful for dressing-up include bits of old, clean curtains, handbags, scarves, long skirts, safety pins, a crown. It is unnecessary to have anything elaborate. The children themselves will choose and adapt what they need. They may start some acting themselves, e.g., playing at "houses." "You be the daddy and I'll be the mummy and John the baby." Sometimes the theme may be suggested by a story told by the teacher and at other times the teacher herself may discuss a story or incident with the children and plan with them a dramatic presentation of it. The children make up the dialogue as they go along and it is not necessary for the teacher to suggest words to them. Where stories, in which Jesus is the main character, are dramatised, the children should still be allowed to choose the part they wish to play. At this stage children quite naturally play the part of Jesus and the teacher should *not* step in to prevent them.

A corner of the hall or a corridor space is more suitable than a stage or platform for this kind of dramatisation. The aim is for the children to participate, not to watch a performance.

PUPPETS

Puppets can be made by the children to illustrate a number of stories and they should be simple enough for the children to make without too much direction from the teacher.

Stick puppets, using the children's own drawings, paper bag and match-box puppets and puppets made from various kinds of scrap materials are easily made. (*Growing Up in the Church, First Year,* pp. 30-31, and *Second Year,* pp. 23-24.) Puppets made from yogurt cartons and wooden spoons are suggested with the appropriate themes in this volume.

The teacher should show the children how to make the puppets, perhaps showing them one she has made, but the children should be allowed to use their own imagination as much as possible. The opportunity to make and use puppets appeals to most children and quite often the child who does not want to take part in the dramatisation will enjoy using a puppet. The great value of a puppet at this stage is not so much in the making as in the using of it. Puppets provide a valuable alternative to dramatic play in a crowded department. No elaborate theatre is necessary as the children quickly improvise their own with a chair, a large cardboard carton or a picture frame.

WORKSHEETS

The worksheets are an "optional" extra and should never be given a dominant place in the activities. The danger is that teachers may be tempted to use them, because of their convenience, to the detriment of the more satisfying creative activities. Although children can work at this activity without much help from the teacher, a teacher should be available to help and guide those children who need it. Often the space in the worksheet is too small for the children to draw their picture (this is especially true of the younger section). Large sheets of paper (size 12" x 8") and coloured wax crayons should always be available so that these children can extend the work suggested by the worksheet. Each worksheet covers one theme and is therefore applicable for that time. It may then be taken home, thus acting as a link with the parents and extending the child's interest in the theme into the home.

BOOK CORNER

Suitable books are suggested with each theme for the children to use in the Book Corner and a supply of books can be built up gradually.

The corner should be as attractive as possible and small tables and chairs, a rug and a book rack are useful equipment. The children should be free to use this corner during the activity time either as an additional activity or for reference. One of the teachers might read a story from a selected book to any children who are interested but this should not be imposed on them by an adult.

WONDER TABLE

There is a place in the Primary for the wonder table on which objects can be placed to stimulate the child's wonder and curiosity. It is particularly relevant to the harvest and summer themes when a display is set up to which the children can contribute. The objects should be displayed attractively on a low table and the children given the opportunity to look, listen, smell, touch and sometimes taste the various articles.

**Planning a
practical project**

Concern for others is often expressed through a practical project in which the children are encouraged to share in this aspect of the Church's ministry. A project must meet a real need of real people and the children must be led to see the need and share in the planning of the project with their teachers. For the children to take an active part in making, collecting and distributing the gifts the project must not make demands beyond their capability. Giving has more meaning when it arises from the experiences of the group. Perhaps Gordon has been ill for a long time; the group plan and make a box of toys and games to send him.

Margaret's granny is blind and so the group take her a bowl of hyacinths which she can smell, even though she can't see them.

Before engaging in such a project, the teachers should always check that the gifts will be welcomed.

**Helping
children to
choose**

Most children find it easy to choose which activity they wish to pursue but there are always individual children who need special help. Carol, a very shy, timid child would not choose, she just sat on her chair watching the other children. The leader allowed her to do this for a few weeks before assigning one of the young helpers to look after her during the activity time. Every week the helper took Carol to each of the activity groups in turn, talked with her about the things the children were making or doing and encouraged her to try out some of the materials. Only after a number of weeks of this individual help was Carol ready to choose one of the activities herself.

There are many reasons why children cannot choose an activity. Some are timid and afraid of unfamiliar materials, others are quite clearly "put off" by the attitudes of their parents. Roger said, "My mummy says I mustn't get my hands dirty" and would never choose painting or any activity where he needed to use glue. The importance of these learning activities should be pointed out to parents either informally when the occasion arises or at a parent-teacher meeting. The twins John and Jennifer choose to do worksheets every week for months, in spite of the efforts of their teacher to persuade them to try some other activity. Later their mother commented to the teacher that at home the twins had said, "Miss Robb is always asking us if we would like to act, or paint, or help to make a model, but we *like* doing the worksheets." When children are given a choice of materials they should be allowed to continue an activity as long as their interest or need for it exists. They may be gaining confidence by experimenting with familiar material or they may be so engrossed in it that they want to explore all the possibilities. The teacher might suggest other activities but she should not be anxious if the children persist at one activity and should certainly not prevent them from doing so. The children usually know themselves when they are ready to choose another activity.

USE OF TIME

On most Sundays the Primary hour will be divided in the following way:
  15 mins.—Worship in the church with the congregation
  10 mins.—Theme introduced by story or informal talk in class groups
  20 mins.—A choice of activities
   5 mins.—Clearing away time
  10 mins.—Closing worship in the Primary room

WORKING WITH LARGE NUMBERS

In Primaries with about fifty children the room can be arranged so that the children have a completely free choice of activities but with larger numbers the hall might be divided into two or four sections with at least four activities in each section. The suggested layout (see Fig. 1) is used by a large Primary of one hundred children, with ten teachers, the leader, an assistant leader and four teachers in training. The hall is of average size, with a platform at one end. The children are divided into younger and older sections with five classes in each. The activities are arranged so that children in each section have a choice of six activities which vary with each theme. The platform is used for two older section class groups and for two "quieter" activities.

Improvising equipment

Where numbers are large and storage difficult, every available space must be utilised and some equipment may have to be improvised. In this Primary, hooks attached to the wall at a height of 3 ft. are available in two corners of the hall for hanging up the dressing-up materials and dramatisation takes place either in these corners or in the corridor spaces rather than on the platform. Occasionally, during the activity time, a small group gathers round the piano to learn some new songs.

A book rack has been attached to the back of the piano for displaying books and mats are available for a group of children to sit on as they look at books. Tables for painting, model-making and the wonder table are hinged to the wall at a height of 2 ft. and let down when not in use. The other tables for activity groups are stackable but these can also be improvised by placing pieces of five-ply wood 4 ft. x 2 ft. on two adult chairs.

Large pieces of "Cellotex" have been fixed to the wall, at the right eye level for Primary children, for displaying posters and the children's work.

For the closing worship, the class groups remain but the children turn their chairs to face the leader's table and the two groups who meet on the platform sit on mats at the side of this table.

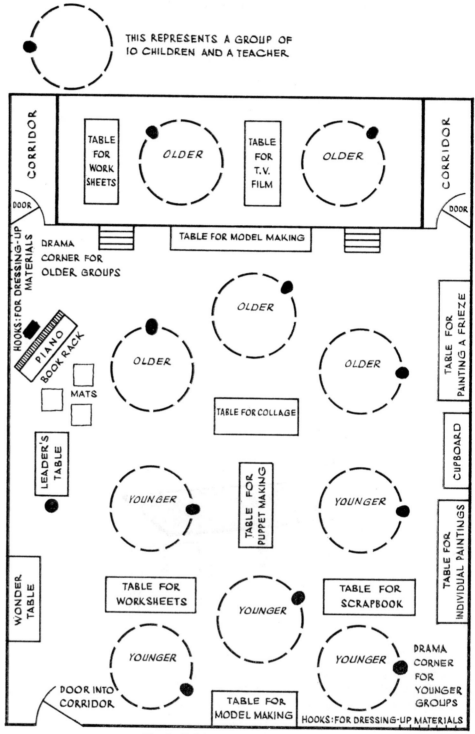

Fig. 1. Hall layout for a large Primary.

WORKING IN THE RURAL PRIMARY

The layout given in Fig. 2 is used by a small Primary of sixteen children, one teacher, the leader and a young helper. The only accommodation available is the church itself and, therefore, one corner of it has been adapted to meet the needs of the Primary. Two pews have been taken out and placed along the wall and another has been reversed. The seats of these pews then form the tables for the activities. A cupboard has been built under one of the pews for storing equipment. The back of the piano is used for displaying posters and children's work and an easel has been made for painting. The children are divided into two groups; the leader introducing the stories and talks to the older section and the teacher to the younger section. The organisation of the activities is shared by the leader and teacher and usually a choice of four or five activities is given each week.

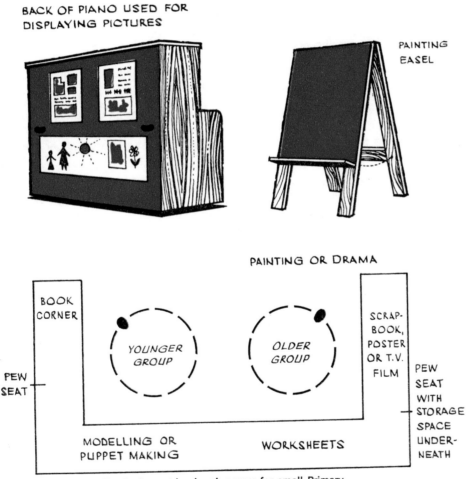

Fig. 2. Layout in church corner for small Primary.

BASIC MATERIALS FOR THE PRIMARY ROOM

The following list of basic materials for creative activities is for a group of 30 to 50 children for one year. The amount of material used will depend on the choice of activities provided by the teachers. It is best to keep these supplies in a cupboard that can be locked. If they are arranged neatly on shelves, which are labelled appropriately, they can be returned easily to their proper place after use.

Paper

Newsprint 18″ x 24″; sugar paper; rolls of wallpaper; shelf or frieze paper; brown wrapping paper; newspaper; old magazines and catalogues.

Paint

Powder colour (one tin of each); white, black, blue, red, yellow, green; two stacking palettes or bun tins of "Opake" colour cakes or "Tempera" blocks, plus two sets of refills; paper towels or paint rags; one dozen long-handled paint brushes, sizes 8, 10 and 12; half a dozen painting aprons.

Crayons

Four packets of Freart or Chubbi-stumps wax crayons; four packets of Finart wax crayons; one dozen felt pens; one dozen large pencils (Rowney's "Black Beauty" or Venus "Black Magic").

Scissors

One dozen small scissors, $4\frac{1}{2}$″ size; one large pair.

Adhesives

"Polycel," "Gloy Multiglue"; brown gummed paper; a stapler; paper fasteners; string; sellotape; one dozen paste brushes.

Modelling material

Plasticine; clay; "play-doh" or flour and salt dough; an unlimited supply of cardboard cartons and scraps of material.

Drawing pins; pipe-cleaners; clothes-pegs; elastic bands; paper towels; waste paper basket.

Books

The supply of books for the Book Corner will be built up gradually throughout the year. Some will be made by the teachers and children, others selected from the list of suggestions given with each theme.

A collage picture or frieze is made of scraps of material of various colours, shapes and textures (see page 24).

Children enjoy painting (see page 23).

Natural gas being flared off aboard the
drilling rig "Orion" in the North Sea (see page 61).

Cutting and stacking peat on the Isle of Skye (see page 61).

(Photo: Maurice Broomfield; Courtesy: The Gas Council)

(Photo: Scottish Tourist Board)

Harvesting rice in India.

(Photo: Unations)

WORSHIP

Primary children are being nurtured within a worshipping community, therefore, as they grow up, they should learn to worship. There are two necessary aspects of worship they should encounter at the Primary stage. One is sharing in worship with the whole congregation as part of the family of the church. The other is worship which arises naturally and spontaneously from the themes explored and the experiences shared in the Primary room, and expressed in language and concepts related to the child's own everyday life.

Wherever possible, the Primary should begin in church, with the children attending a short part of the service. The children should be encouraged to sit with their parents and any who are unaccompanied can either sit with a "church friend" (this may be a teacher or an adult in the church who has invited a small group of children to sit with them) or they can be incorporated in other family groups so that they, too, feel part of the congregation. Sitting with adults in a family group encourages the children to focus their attention on what is happening in the service, helps them to participate, and to feel part of the congregation.

In the church

Where local circumstances prevent the children from attending the church service every week, arrangements should be made for them to visit the church on special occasions to share in part of the service and to know that they are part of the Church.

"The attitude of reverence towards God, which is the basis of all worship, is caught rather than taught, therefore, children, in particular, learn to worship by being with a congregation whose worship is real." Although much of the worship in church may be beyond the child's immediate understanding, he is learning by being there. He becomes familiar with the building, meets the people, observes the things they do, and begins to take his place within the worshipping family of God. During the Primary programme, as he works at projects, and has an opportunity to talk with some of the people of the church about the things they do in the church, he grows in his own understanding of worship.

The child grows in his understanding of worship

As indicated in *Growing Up in the Church—Second Year*, if the Lord's prayer is used in church during the part of the service the Primary attends, then the children should be helped to learn it in the Primary. A possible objection is that the words may have little meaning for the child at this stage. But this is to miss the point. Worship is itself a learning experience: the children learn by doing. The child learns much by participation, even before the meaning of the words used becomes clear to him. The child attends church worship to participate in it with the whole family of God's people, and he will learn its meaning gradually as he grows up. Primary worship is designed to relate the life of the child to God and to prepare him for fuller participation in church worship.[1]

The Lord's Prayer

[1] *Growing Up in the Church, Second Year*, p. 29.

B*

In the Primary

As the children leave church to go to the Primary, they should do so quietly, while the organist plays; at the end of the hymn, rather than during the singing of it. To leave during a hymn does not help the children to appreciate the place of hymns in worship.

It is usually the responsibility of the Primary leader to conduct worship in the Primary, although the initial planning may be done in co-operation with all the teachers, at the preparation class. When the Primary children attend the beginning of the church service, this should be regarded as the opening act of worship for the Primary. The children should then meet immediately in their class groups when they go into the Primary room. The closing act of worship should be brief, informal and enjoyable. Usually not more than two short hymns, or part of a hymn, a short prayer and one or two verses from the Bible will be used.

Related to experience

Worship in which the children engage at the Primary level is not an imitation of adult worship, and we must be careful not to confuse the children with adult words and concepts which are quite outwith their experience. This does not mean that hymns and Bible readings must never be used unless every thought and word is understood; this would limit the scope of worship too much. If worship is to be real to the children it must grow from their experience, and should lead on from what is already known to a fuller understanding.

The most appropriate time for worship in the Primary is after the activities; when pictures children have painted, discoveries they have made, experiences they have enjoyed and prayers they have written are gathered together. While some of the children help to tidy away the materials and display their work, others arrange the chairs in informal groups facing the worship centre, ready for the brief act of worship.

The *worship centre* consists of a table covered with an attractive cloth (preferably one the children have helped to make), an open copy of the Revised Standard Version of the Bible, the offering plates and perhaps a vase of flowers.

Hymns

Suggestions of suitable hymns, Bible readings and prayers are provided with each theme. Where there is an appropriate "hymn for the theme," this might be used each Sunday to enable the children to sing it well. All the hymns should be chosen carefully to ensure that they are bright, lively, and meaningful to the child. Children often misinterpret the words of hymns, but this should stimulate us to provide hymns more suited to their experience and understanding. The hymns in the Primary must help the child to express his relationship to God through his experiences of the world around him (e.g., home, friends, school, nature, church) in praise and thanksgiving; and help him to participate more fully in worship in the church.

Even young children enjoy the great hymns of the Church, especially those containing repetition in which they can join without being familiar with all the words, e.g., "All creatures of our God and King." Selected verses or just the chorus of some of these hymns are not too difficult for Primary children to learn. The hymns may be accompanied by piano, guitar, recorder or other instrument, and occasionally the children may participate with percussion instruments, triangles, tambourines, drums, castanets, bells and cymbals, some of which can be improvised and made by the children. (See *The Church Nursery Group*, pp. 23-24.)

The learning of new hymns and the practice of familiar ones is an activity quite distinct from the worship period. It can be taken either with a small group gathered round the piano as one of the choices during the other activities or with the whole group in the few minutes preceding the worship. A new tune should be played through several times, perhaps as listening music while the offering is uplifted, then sung by the leader or one of the staff before asking the children to sing it. The words of the hymn need to be memorised but the whole stanza should be repeated a number of times rather than line by line. The hymn then has coherence and the children see the pattern and grasp the meaning more readily. Obviously the leader and teachers must become thoroughly familiar with the words and music at the preparation class before introducing a new hymn to the children.

A large illustrated hymn sheet, with the words printed in large letters with a felt-tipped pen and illustrated either by pictures the children have drawn or cut from magazines helps the children to memorise the words and to understand the meaning as they learn. Older Primary children, who are able to read, might make their own illustrated hymn book, or hymn card, as an activity. A large book containing a number of hymns illustrated by the children would be a useful addition to the Book Corner.

Some children enjoy helping to write new words to a familiar tune. The children might be given an opportunity to do this for themes for which there are very few appropriate hymns. The rhyme does not matter, but the children's ideas are important and these can be preserved even if the lines need to be re-formed by the teacher. Tunes most suitable for the writing of new hymns are "Frère Jacques" (p. 164) ; "Praise to God for things we see" (p. 159) ; and "Let us sing our song of praise" (*Hymns for Younger Children*).

It is easier to teach children to "say a prayer" than it is to help them to pray. "The only effective way of praying with children is born out of a real relationship with them, developed through working and playing together, through conversation and sharing."[1] Prayers should be short and specific, dealing with concrete needs and experiences of the child and, like the hymns, should use language and concepts that are meaningful to him. In other words, they must be about things that are *real* to the child. *Thanksgiving* is the most natural form of prayer for the young child and prayers of thanksgiving for particular things they enjoy fit best into the experience of Primary children. Prayers of *supplication* in which we ask God's help for ourselves also have a place in the Primary provided they are brief, e.g., "Help us to share our toys with others." The prayer of *confession* is furthest removed from the child's experience at this stage and should be used sparingly. Prayers of *intercession* for others, especially those the children know themselves, give expression to the attitude of compassion and care for others that we wish to encourage. The leader should vary the forms of prayers rather than asking the children to repeat the prayer phrase by phrase every week. A litany, where the leader says phrases such as : "For the big juicy Jaffa oranges that come to us from Israel" ; and the children respond, "We thank you, O God" after each phrase, is an easy form for Primary children.

Learning hymns

PRAYERS

[1] D. R. Wilton, *Praying with Primaries.*

A short prayer, using not more than two kinds of prayers mentioned above, in which the children are asked to listen while the leader says the words, is another useful form.

Teachers can help a child or a group of children to formulate their ideas in a prayer during the activities. These prayers might be written out by the children and made into "Our Book of Prayers" to be used in the Book Corner. Occasionally, the leader might use one of these prayers during the act of worship.

The following books may help the leader as she plans the Primary worship:

> *Prayer for Younger Children*, by Brenda Holloway
> *Praying with Primaries*, by D. R. Wilton
> *Please God*, by Beryl Bye and Joyce Badrocke

Using the Bible

The Bible has a place in Primary worship and it is important for the children to observe it in use in the church and in the Primary. A copy of the Bible, attractively bound and illustrated with pictures of people, places and things that are interesting to the children, should be on display on the worship table. It should be accessible throughout the session and the children should be encouraged to look at it.

The teacher's attitude to the Bible and the care with which she handles it is vital at this stage when the child's early attitudes are being formed. The child begins to sense that the Bible is important to his teacher and he learns to treat it carefully, too. The Bible will be used incidentally as the occasion arises, for instance, during a conversation with Sandra about the snow looking like cotton wool, the teacher was able to read "He gives snow like wool" (Ps. 147 : 16a) and at this point the verse from the Bible was relevant to the child's experience. Biblical language is difficult for young children and the version of the Bible we use is important. Perhaps the most suitable is the Revised Standard Version and it is recommended throughout this programme. Selected Bible verses which relate to the themes are suggested for the guidance of the leader and they should be used in a meaningful way rather than read as verses isolated from the child's experience. Examples are given with each theme to show how the verses might be incorporated naturally so that they are appropriate to the children's interest or activity.

Offering

As suggested in *Growing Up in the Church—First Year:* "When the offering is taken, children should uplift it as the elders do in church. They should bring it forward to the worship table and lay it upon it. During the offering, music should be played (as in church). The leader should explain that this is a 'listening time.' Music may be played on piano, guitar or similar instrument or on a record player, thus eliminating the choruses which have frequently been sung at this point."[1] Alternatively, the offering may be collected as the children enter and placed on the worship table as music is played, during the act of worship. If a dedicatory prayer is used it should be specific and in words the children understand, such as: "We thank you, O God, that we are well and strong and can run about and play. Some of the boys and girls in Southern Yemen are sick. We bring our gifts so that they may have medicine to make them well again."

[1] *Growing Up in the Church First Year* p. 37. *(cf) Second Year*, p. 31

Music

Recorded music can be used to create the atmosphere as the children gather for the act of worship and while the offering is being uplifted. For this, a good record player, or tape recorder, is necessary. It is particularly valuable in a large department or where the pianist is not able to extemporise. Where music is appropriate to the theme (see Theme 7) it can be used during the activities, not as background music, but for a group of children to listen to or for telling a story through movement and dance. Sometimes the story in movement and dance created by a group of children can be incorporated in the act of worship but care should be taken to ensure that it is part of the worship and not a performance.

Preparation

To lead boys and girls in worship is difficult and needs careful thought and preparation which cannot, and indeed must not, be done in the few minutes before the service is due to begin. But, of course, this careful planning must not rule out any spontaneous moments of worship that arise during the session. The experience of wonder, which is one aspect of worship, may occur at any time, and the teacher must be sensitive to this. As a child or a group of children examine a flower, or listen to the noise in a seashell, their sense of wonder can sometimes be expressed in a short prayer but at other times it is sufficient for the teacher to share the child's wonder.

A shared experience

The attitude of the teachers to worship is all-important, for they cannot hope to help children to worship unless they worship God themselves. Children quickly sense the difference between an activity which is imposed upon them by the teachers and one in which they all share. But when all the activities, thoughts, and experiences shared by teachers and children are offered to God in the hymns, prayers and readings, worship becomes a natural part of the whole session.

PREPARING TO TEACH

The importance of preparation

The success of any programme depends on the amount of planning and preparation the leader and teachers are prepared to give to it. Teaching in Sunday school involves far more than attendance for one hour on a Sunday morning, and preparation is a principle that is accepted by all who undertake this work.

The teacher is the representative of the whole congregation, fulfilling for them their responsibility towards those who are entrusted to her care. Obviously she must know the material she is going to use with the children, and this section is designed to help the teacher in her preparation of it. In addition, she must deepen her understanding of the child, be aware of the role of the Primary in the life of the Church, and be growing in her own faith as a Christian.

Teachers plan together

The Primary leader and her staff will meet together to prepare at least once a month, although more frequent meetings would be desirable. Teachers who prepare together gain a great deal from the experience and find that their own personal faith is enriched when the study of the themes is shared with others. Regular attendance should be regarded by every teacher as of paramount importance and where teachers are accustomed to a regular preparation class they would not want to do without them. The leader is responsible for arranging the meeting but she should try to avoid dominating the group. Rather she should encourage the teachers to make their own contributions and share fully in the planning of the themes. When the leader is arranging the night for the group to meet, she should choose the one that suits the majority of the staff. Arrangements sometimes have to be made for the leader to give individual help to a teacher, who, for a good reason, cannot attend.

Every teacher must realise that the success of the department depends on the working together of a team. The whole atmosphere for learning in the Primary largely depends on how well the teachers work together and share the responsibilities. Where teachers are prepared to work together and make the most of their situation, successful teaching can take place even under difficult conditions. In some churches, where two Primary groups use the same hall at different times, there must be co-operation and careful planning by the staff of both groups to ensure that the accommodation, equipment and time are used in the best possible way.

AT THE PREPARATION CLASS

The theme that is to be used on the following four or five Sundays will be the main concern of the preparation class. Each teacher should bring with her a copy of the Revised Standard Version of the Bible, the resource book, *Growing Up in the Church*, and a notebook.

Teachers learn

A careful study of the section "Preparing for the Theme" will enable teachers to understand the aim of the theme, what their approach to it should be and the significance of the Biblical foundations which underlie it.

Most ministers are willing to help with the study of the Bible passages. In addition, they may be glad to have an opportunity to discuss with the teachers the work of the Sunday school.

A look at the theme in outline will enable the teachers to get a picture of the entire theme and how it develops over the four weeks, rather than seeing each week as an isolated unit. In this way the aim will be seen more clearly and the appropriate emphasis can be made.

Stories and talks

The stories and talks which have been read carefully by the teachers *before* the preparation class should be discussed and the difficult points considered. Teachers might be asked to take turns at introducing one of the stories. If the teachers feel that the story will be too familiar for the children and that they will be greeted with "We've heard that before," then they must consider whether it is advisable to encourage the children to recall the story by answering appropriate questions. It might also be necessary to consider which of the stories the teachers should tell in their own words and which should be read. Teachers might help each other with the approach to the informal talk, the more experienced teachers offering suggestions to those who may be having difficulties.

The stories and talks are sometimes provided in two forms, a simpler form for the five and younger six-year-olds and a more advanced form for the six-plus and seven-year-olds. Teachers who are in charge of a group of six-year-olds may sometimes find it necessary to consider which of the two forms they should use.

Activities

The story, or talk, serves merely as an introduction to the theme. The teachers should therefore discuss which activities will best help the children to explore the theme imaginatively and creatively and plan accordingly. The arrangement of the room should be planned and each teacher should know which activity she is to be responsible for organising, so that she can begin to collect together the materials the children will require. For example, if she is responsible for organising the painting group she must see that there is sufficient paper cut to the appropriate sizes—some ready for a frieze and some for individual paintings—and that the paints are clean and mixed to the right consistency. A teacher who has not been able to attend the preparation class can be assigned to guide the children who choose to do worksheets, to supervise the children using the Book Corner, or to assist a teacher whose activity requires the help of more than one adult.

After a time, some teachers may want to "specialise" in organising one particular activity. However good a practice this may appear to be, the leader should encourage all the teachers to be adaptable and to be able to take their turn with any of the activities.

As many teachers have not had the opportunity of using the creative materials themselves, they should experiment with some of the suggested activities at the preparation class. This will enable them to discover both the possibilities and the difficulties involved

Primary worship

Although worship in the Primary is mainly the concern of the Primary leader, all the teachers might be involved in the planning of it. Several hymns are suggested with each theme and the teachers should know them and learn any new ones before the leader introduces them to the children. (Where the children meet for the first part of morning worship in the church, arrangements might be made for one of the hymns to be included in the service.) The Bible readings and prayers might also receive the attention of the group.

Finally, there should always be time available for the staff to look at the work they have covered in the previous theme; to see what has been of value, to discuss the reactions of the children and any difficulties that were encountered and to consider improvements that may be necessary for the efficiency of the department.

Time will invariably be too short in one meeting for all the preparation that is necessary, but if teachers have read through the entire theme before meeting together much more will be accomplished.

INDIVIDUAL PREPARATION

Look ahead

The work of preparation by the whole Primary staff will be made much easier if the teachers can do some individual preparation beforehand. In this way they will be better able to contribute their own ideas and suggest the names of those who might help in particular tasks.

At the beginning of the session a teacher should read the introduction to the resource book and then through the themes, getting a general picture of the programme she will be covering throughout the session. She may find it useful to make a note of any pictures, photographs and materials she will need and also any ideas that occur to her as she reads, ready for discussion with the other teachers at the preparation classes. If the teacher is not already a hoarder, the instinct develops quickly, as she collects cartons for the model-making, scraps of fabric for the collage and puppets and pieces of material for the dramatisation!

Every week

The teacher should start to prepare early in the week. She should not leave it until the last minute and, preferably, should set aside a specific time each week for preparation. The story or talk will be read with her own particular group in mind. Whether the story is told or read to the group will depend on the story itself and the children, but in either case the teacher will need to be thoroughly familiar with it. Any pictures and materials required for the activities need to be gathered and supplies of glue or paint checked, and if necessary replenished, before the final preparation of the Primary room on Sunday morning.

The words of any new hymns should either be learned by heart or copied into a notebook.

Finally, the teacher should commend the work she is preparing to do and the children in her group to God, asking for his help and guidance.

TRAINING NEW TEACHERS

Recruitment

There are two main sources for the supply of teachers. The first is the Communicants' class. When the prospective Communicants have reached the end of the course, in which they have studied the various aspects of the Christian faith, and discovered for themselves that they want to join in the fellowship of the Church, they may find themselves challenged to become involved in this form of service. The second source is the young mothers in the congregation, particularly those whose children are not in the Primary department. These women often make good Primary teachers because of their greater maturity and experience. The approach to such people is best made by the personal invitation of the minister.

Young staff should only be used as helpers and they should always be given adequate training and support. The place for the new teacher to begin her practical training is as a helper in the Primary department, rather than in the Nursery, or Junior departments. Primary children are not so demanding and are more responsive, and so are more easily handled by the inexperienced teacher. The length of time that a person remains as a helper before recognition as a teacher will depend upon her age, the progress she makes in training and her relationships with the children. For the first few months in the department, the teacher in training should sit with one of the experienced teachers, watching her at work with her class and helping her with one of the activity groups. Later, after she has received some training, the helper should be given the opportunity of telling the story or introducing the informal talk, with the experienced teacher there to give help and assurance.

Teachers in training

The need for training new teachers has always been recognised as of vital importance by those concerned with Christian education. The effectiveness of the Sunday school depends on whether new teachers are trained and whether those already involved in teaching are prepared to be continually learning about their work. Training is provided by the Church on national and area levels but the local church or group of churches can supplement these courses by providing a course themselves. The Christian Education Group within the local church might be responsible for the organisation of a course of training, but where this is impracticable the Primary leader should take the initiative. The following outline is given as a basis for those who plan such a course of training, using the three volumes of *Growing Up in the Church*.

A training course

A Programme of Christian Education (1st week)

Part I

  (a) Basic principles—Third year, pp. 9-10.
  (b) Christian nurture—The young child in the church—First year, pp. 11-14.
  (c) The place of the congregation—Second year, pp. 32-38; Third year, pp. 11-13.
      (A visit should be arranged for new teachers to see each department of the Sunday school in operation.)

The Primary Child (2nd, 3rd and 4th weeks)

Part II

  (a) The characteristics and needs of the Primary child—First year, pp. 16-17; Second year, pp. 38-42; Third year, pp. 14-17.
  (b) How the child learns—First year, pp. 17-18; Third year, pp. 16-17.
  (c) Relationships: The teacher and the child—Second year, p. 15.
      The Groups—Third year, pp. 18-19.
  (c) The Primary in operation—Second year, pp. 9-13; First year, pp. 19-20.

B**

Part III

Communicating with the Primary child (5th, 6th and 7th weeks)

  (a) The themes: related to the child and selection of material—Second year, pp. 18-19; 43-45; Third year, p. 18.

  (b) Stories and informal talks—First year, p. 21; Second year—p. 18; Third year, pp. 19-21.

     (Prepare a story or informal talk ready to introduce to a class group the following Sunday.)

  (c) Activities—First year, pp. 22-34; 39-41; Second year, pp. 19-28; Third year, pp. 22-28.

     (Experiment with creative materials and prepare materials ready for a group activity the following Sunday.)

  (d) Worship—As part of the whole Church—First year, p. 19; Second year, p. 16; Third year, p. 33.

     In the Primary room—First year, pp. 34-37; Second year, pp. 28-31; Third year, pp. 34-37.

Part IV

The preparation of teacher (8th week)

  (a) The preparation class in operation—First year, p. 38.

  (b) Preparing to teach—Third year, pp. 38-41.

THE PRIMARY TEACHERS' LIBRARY

The following books are recommended as the basis of a Primary Teachers' Library.

Lilian Hollamby, *Young Children Living and Learning*, Longmans.

E. M. Matterson, *Play with a Purpose for under Sevens*, Penguin.

L. G. W. Sealer and V. Gibbon, *Communication and Learning in the Primary School*, Basil Blackwell, Oxford.

Violet Madge, *Children in Search of Meaning*, S.C.M. Press.

F. & P. Cliff, *A Diary of Teachers of Infants*, Ruper Hart-Davies.

R. S. Lee, *Your Growing Child and Religion*, Penguin.

D. Simpson and D. M. Alderson, *Creative Play in the Infant School*, Pitman.

N. Isaacs, *The Growth of Understanding in the Young Child*, Ward Lock.

Working with Primaries, N.C.E.C.

Renee Seville, *Beginning Arts & Crafts*, Evans Bros.

Violet Madge, *Introducing Young Children to Jesus*, S.C.M. Press.

One Hundred Exciting Things to Do, Deans.

Brenda Holloway, *Prayers for Younger Children*, University of London Press.

Beryl Bye and Joyce Badrocke, *Please God . . . Prayers for Children*, Falcon.

D. R. Wilton, *Praying with Primaries*, N.C.E.C.

M. Kitson and G. Foote, *Infant Praise*, Evans Bros.

The New English Bible.

Alan T. Dale, *New World*, Oxford University Press.

Brian Galliers, *Go . . . Teach*, N.C.E.C.

Each teacher should possess her own copy of the Revised Standard Version of the Bible.

1 Belonging

PREPARING FOR THIS THEME

This theme is designed to be the first theme of the session when the children return after the summer holidays. In some churches where the harvest thanksgiving service takes place in September, the material for the harvest theme may need to be used first but as the material is undated adjustments can be made to suit local circumstances.

TIME OF YEAR

The theme begins by encouraging the children to talk about themselves and their families. The family is the most significant belonging-group the child has experience of; it is his earliest environment and the relationships made within this group affect his ability to make contact with others and also his ability to appreciate the care of God. As the theme develops the children are encouraged to talk about belonging to other groups; their friends at home and at school. Finally, as they experience something of belonging to their Sunday school group, they are helped to see that they belong to the Church family.

APPROACH TO THEME

Families are part of God's provision for us. He does not intend that we should live alone, but has given us these natural groups to which we belong and in whose security we may develop. (See Gen. 2 : 18 and 4 : 1.) He intends that husband and wife shall love and be faithful to each other throughout their life and that children should be born and brought up surrounded by love. It is through the parents that the love of God first reaches them.

BIBLICAL FOUNDATIONS

The family

Read Luke 15: 11-32. The story which Jesus told to illustrate the constancy of God's love shows a loving father seeking a complete reconciliation within the family and indicates the responsibility of members of a family for the well-being of the group. In Matt. 7: 8, 9 and 21 : 28-29, Jesus recognises the duties of parents to children and children to parents. Look up Eph. 5 : 21-6 : 4 for a summary of family duties in the light of Christian experience. The Fatherhood of God sets the pattern for and strengthens the human family (see Eph. 3 : 14).

Mutual responsibility

The human family is not, however, to control our lives, and our first loyalty is to God who calls us into a new family which is his Church.
Read Mark 3: 31-35 and Matt. 10: 29-30 and 35-38. Family ties must not deprive us of the privilege of belonging to the family or household of God.
John Calvin speaks of the Church as the mother of those whose Father is God, and this family conception of the Church has been strong since its earliest days. Look up 2 John : 4-6, 13.

The church family

Read 1 John 4: 7-21. All human relationships are affected by the relationship we have with God. Those who call him "Father" must seek to bear the family likeness, and his generous love to them will enable them to show an out-going

The outlook of the Christian family

43

love like his own. Primary children are being nurtured within the church family and as they are shown God's love by the adults they meet they will be helped to respond to others in love and begin to bear this family likeness.

PRIMARY WORSHIP

The hymn for the theme might be Infant Praise (I.P. 35) "Let us thank the Heavenly Father." Other appropriate hymns and songs are: "Our friends and our families," p. 164 ("Happy Thought," verse 2) ; "To God who makes all lovely things" (I.P. 13) 1 and 5; "Sing a glad song" (I.P. 38) ; "Children, Come !" p. 163; "At Church," p. 159.

The section on Primary Worship on p. 34 will help the leader as she plans the worship in the department.

Bible readings—When the verses from the Bible are read, a short but relevant introduction is usually required. For instance, for the third week of this theme the leader might say : "You are all learning new things and making new friends at school. Jesus went to school, too. Here is a verse from the Bible that he had to learn at school." Read Deut. 6 : 4 and 5.

Other Bible readings for this theme might be—John 15 : 12 and 14 ; Ps. 100 : 4 and Ps. 122 : 1.

Prayers—Prayers of thanksgiving for families and friends are appropriate. Prayers that the children write themselves about their families and the games they play with their friends might be made into a book of prayers to be used during the Primary worship.

THE THEME IN OUTLINE

First week: "I belong to my family."

I feel at home ; I feel comfortable and safe ; I can be myself amongst others ; I don't want to hurt these people, they are too precious to me ; I don't like it when they hurt me ; I don't want it to change.

These are childish responses expressed in adult terms for the guidance of the teachers. The informal talk will expand these "feelings" so that the children can enter into it with some reality.

Second week: "I belong to my friends."

I like to be with them ; I like to imitate them ; I like to play with them ; I feel good when I'm with them ; I feel strong when I'm with them ; there are some I like and some I don't like ; I don't want them to put me out ; I don't want anyone to spoil it for us.

These responses, again expressed in adult terms, are only intended to give a "picture" of the child in this situation. In the informal talk these ideas will be expanded when the children themselves will give the lead. The teacher must listen for the important phrases the children use about being with their friends.

Third week: "I belong to my class at school."

I feel grown up; I am clever because I am at school; I would like to be strong amongst these other children; I like my teacher/I don't like my teacher; I have some of my friends around me; we have our own room and books; we play together here.

This is a totally different kind of "belonging" to either of the others, mainly because it is a *purposeful* group, and also because it tends to be focused on one adult, the teacher.

Again let the children take the lead, using the above responses as a guide to the kind of things they *might* say in their own words. It is *their experience* we are talking about, not what we think it ought to be. The teacher can learn a lot about her children by listening to them.

Fourth week: "I belong to the Church."

The informal talk this week is the exploration by *the children* within the real group to which they now belong. It encourages them to talk about the things they do at home on Sundays and about the things they do together in Sunday school and church. The story about Anne's baptism introduces them to the idea that even the tiny babies that are baptised belong to the family of the church.

Suggestions for the Book Corner

Helping at Home, Shopping with Mother, Going to School, Our Friends,
    Play with Us, Fun and Games (Ladybird Books).
Topsy and Tim at School (Blackie).

WEEK BY WEEK THROUGH THE THEME

"BELONGING TO THE FAMILY"

FIRST WEEK

Note for teachers

The following passage is an expansion of the responses suggested in the theme in outline and a description of the type of questioning and answering that might take place in the course of a session of this kind. Since this is the first week of the new session and new groups have been formed, this is an appropriate time for teacher and children to share experiences so that a good relationship is established between them. Throughout the informal talk the teacher must take special care where there are present children who do not live in a "normal" home but in a children's home. The teacher should lead in by telling the children about her own family and should use this as a basis for the rest of the discussion.

BOTH SECTIONS
INFORMAL
TALK

Then ask—Who belongs to your family? (*Mother, father, sisters, brothers, other relatives such as aunts, uncles, cousins, grandparents and even great-grandparents.*) If some child has lost a parent or parents or is being cared for in a children's home, foster parents, adopted parents, "aunts" or "uncles" should be accepted as being just as real.

All these people belong to our family, and when we go away, or they go away, we keep in touch with them—How? (*By writing, telephoning, visiting, going for holidays. Even if "auntie" is in America we still care for her and like to hear her news.*)

Because we usually live in one house with our mum, dad, brothers and sisters, we get to know them very well. In fact, "I know lots more about my Mum than about Mrs. Thomson who lives next door." "I know my Mum likes knitting, pink custard and elephants at the zoo." (*The teacher should add examples from her family.*)

"What do your Mum, Dad, sisters and brothers like?"
"What do your Mum, Dad, sisters, and brothers not like?"
("*My Dad doesn't like muddy shoes, dead flowers and empty match-boxes.*")

"What makes you feel happy when you go home?"
"What is nice about being at home?"
(Answers such as these might be expected—"*My Mum's there.*" (Some may say, "*My Mum's never there when I go home;*" in which case the teacher might say something like: "Isn't she there sometimes?" or, "Oh, but she *is* there sometimes.") "*I can watch TV; It is warm; We get our tea; I get sweets; We ride our bicycles; We play with the dog.*")

"What do you like doing at home?"
(*Playing with trains/cars; reading; drawing; talking to Mum and Dad; going to the zoo; watching ships or trains.*)

"What makes you cross at home?"
(*The children will probably take "cross" to mean "upset."*) (*Getting smacked; left alone; not allowed to watch TV; Mum and Dad having a row.*)

"What sort of things make Mummy cross?"
("*When I'm bad; the dog running away; when I quarrel with my big brother.*")

(These questions are included to indicate that we need not avoid the children's negative feeling. They are part of the whole picture.)

The discussion might end with a short prayer of thanksgiving for their families.

In areas where the children do not meet each other regularly during the week, suggest that they bring a photograph of their family to show to each other next week.

Discuss the various activities that are available for the children to choose from before they go to an activity group.

(i) Painting and drawing. The children can either draw or paint a picture of their family. Encourage the children to talk about their painting by saying, "Tell me about your painting." The teacher may then write the *child's* sentence underneath it. The older children who are able to write, can write their own story about their family.

If the children draw group pictures of their family it would be fun to mount the pictures on the walls or on to large pieces of cardboard and have a Family Picture Gallery. Large cardboard cartons might be opened out and used for mounting the pictures so that they stand up around the room.

(ii) Modelling. The children could make models of their houses from shoe boxes or empty cartons. These could be arranged into streets. Clothes-peg, pipe-cleaner or plasticine figures of their family and trees, walls and gardens could be added to the model.

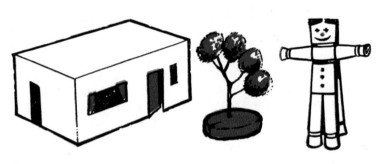

(iii) Role playing. The children might play out the various roles, Mum, Dad, brothers and sisters. Provide various props such as dolls, handbags, cups and saucers, for a house corner. A number of house corners might be set up depending on the size of the department.

(iv) A group scrapbook. Some children could begin a large scrapbook for use during the theme. Today include their writing and pictures about their families. Small individual books can be made in a similar way.

(v) Worksheets. Use can be made of these.

In preparation for the activities next week ask the children to bring one of their toys to share. They might bring things like dolls, cars, balls, skipping ropes, jig-saws.

"BELONGING TO MY FRIENDS"

As in the first week these notes are intended only as a guide.

The teacher should begin the discussion by telling the children something about her own friends.

Then ask: "Who are your friends?" (*Jimmy; the girl next door; Daddy.*)

"How do you know they are your friends?" (*They play with me; we have fun together.*)

"What kind of things do you do together?"

"What games do you play with them?" (*Boys—chasing, football; girls—houses, dolls, skipping.*)

"What is your favourite game?" (*Football, cricket, houses, skipping, dolls.*)

"What happens when someone spoils the game?" (*If someone is nasty, we have a fight, we put him out.*)

(The teacher should avoid adding her own comments if this kind of discussion develops. The aim is to get the children to contribute their own ideas. As there are so many interesting activities it might be advisable to allow as much time as possible for them, but if the teacher has time for a story the following one about two friends may be used.)

"DAVID AND JONATHAN"

David and Jonathan were great friends. They often went out in the fields together to hunt or just to practise shooting with a bow and arrow.

One day Jonathan told David he had heard stories that the king wanted to kill him. "I'll find out if there is anything in it and let you know," he said.

So Jonathan tried to make sure that what he had heard was true. He arranged a secret way of letting David know whether it was safe for him to stay or whether he should run for his life.

"You hide behind this pile of rocks and I will shoot three arrows. If I say to the boy who is with me, 'The arrows are near you,' you will know that you are safe. But if I say, 'The arrows are away beyond you,' you will know you must run for your life."

On the day they had chosen, David hid behind the rocks. Jonathan came into the field with a young boy and his bow and arrows. He shot the arrows, calling, "The arrows are beyond you. You must hurry up and not waste time."

When David heard this he knew he must run away quickly. He waited until the boy who was with Jonathan had gone away before he came out from behind the rocks to say good-bye to his friend. The two friends promised that they would always be ready to help when the other was in trouble. Then David went away.

Many years later David remembered his promise. When he knew that his friend Jonathan had been killed in a battle, he took Jonathan's son into his home and brought him up with his own children.

(i) Playing games. The teacher can find out the favourite games and play them with the group, either indoors or outdoors. There should be an opportunity for playing more than one game.

(ii) Sharing toys. The children who have brought a favourite toy to Sunday school today should be encouraged to share it with some of the others.

(iii) Modelling. The models of the houses begun last week might be continued today.

(iv) Drawing, painting, collage. The children could paint or make pictures of their favourite toys.

(v) The group scrapbook. Include pictures and writing about playing with their friends.

(vi) Worksheets can be used as an additional activity.

"BELONGING TO MY CLASS AT SCHOOL"

THIRD WEEK

Note for teachers

The answers the children give in this week's discussion will vary greatly depending on the children's school district, the day school teacher and the type of school.

In the discussion the Sunday school teacher should try to build up a picture of what the various day school teachers and classrooms are like. The things the children do in school may be very different from the things the teacher did when she went to school.

For this session it would be very helpful if the teacher had a copy of the Ladybird book, "Going to School" or "Topsy and Tim at School" (Blackie).

BOTH SECTIONS
INFORMAL
TALK

"How many of you are back at school after the holidays?" "All of you."
(*The teacher can expect lots of answers such as—"I am at school but my little sister isn't. She's too small"; "I've moved into a new class"; "I've got a new teacher."*)
(In the younger classes there will be children who have just started school and they will have a lot to talk about.)

"What does your school look like?"
"What do you do in school? What do you like doing best?"
"What is your teacher's name? What colour of hair has she?"
Tell me about the things in your classroom. "Have you a big or a little classroom? What number is it? How many children are in your class? What do you sit on? Have you got desks or tables? What do you keep in your desks?"
"Do your friends sit near you in class?"
"Where do you play at play time?" (*In the playground; on the grass.*)
"Do you play with your friends?" "What games do you play?"

Note to teachers   The following story gives an open-ended situation for the children to think out a possible solution. It would be **valuable** if the story could be acted out in the class group so that the children can have experience of the incident.

A STORY PROBLEM

One day Alan and his family moved from their old house in the middle of the big city to a new house in another town.

In his old school he had lots of friends to play with but now in this big new school he knew no-one.

On the first morning in his new class Alan felt very strange and lonely and he missed his friends.

What do you think the children in Alan's class did to make him feel as if he belonged to their class?

What could you do if a new boy or girl came to join your class?

A graph

Before the children leave their class groups let them make a graph of the things they like doing best at school. Two groups might combine if the groups are small.

The teacher should prepare beforehand some small squares of paper of equal size and have sufficient to give one square to each child. On a large piece of paper she should also prepare the lay-out for the graph.

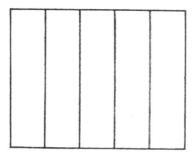

(*a*) Let the children choose five of the activities they like best at school and give each activity a symbol, e.g.:

(*b*) Give each child a square of paper and ask them to draw the symbol for their favourite activity on it.

(*c*) Help them to stick their symbols on to the graph in the appropriate column.

The graph will look something like this when it is finished:

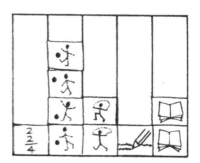

(i) Drawing, painting and collage. The children could draw, paint or make collage pictures of their classroom, or a group could work together and make a large picture of their class.

(ii) Role playing. The children could act out a classroom scene, taking it in turns to be the teacher.

(A house corner, sand tray, book corner, pencils and paper might be included for this group.)

Some children might act out the story problem again.

(iii) The group scrapbook. A group of children could continue with the book, including this week's pictures and writing about "Our school class."

(iv) Use can be made of the worksheets.

"BELONGING TO THE CHURCH"

The kind of discussion that develops this week will depend very much on whether the children's parents attend the church and on whether the Sunday school begins its session in the church. The important thing is for the children to discover something of what it feels like to belong to this group.

Through the activities they should see the "one-ness" of their class, which is a real "belonging."

If the Primary children do not go into the church every Sunday, try to arrange for them to spend a short time in the service during this theme. Arrangements might also be made for them to see the service of baptism in the church.

It will be helpful if the teacher begins the discussion by telling the children something about herself and some of the things she does on Sundays, e.g., long lie; bacon and egg for breakfast.

Then ask, "What happens in your house on Sunday? Who gets up first? Do you have anything different for breakfast?"

"Do your Mummy and Daddy bring you to church or do you come with a friend?"

"What do Mummy and Daddy do while you are here?" (For the purposes of this session it doesn't really matter if they "stay in bed and read the Sunday papers!" Answers will range from "they stay in bed" to "they come to church." We can only hope that some parents do come to church so that this answer may be developed.)

Encourage the children to talk about the things they do together in the Sunday school. (Listen to stories; talk with each other; paint; act; draw; write.)

If the Primary session begins in the church, ask them what they do and see there. (Sing hymns, listen to the Bible being read, see the babies baptised. Mention also the people they see—the minister, church officer, organist and choir.)

STORY

Helen was glad she had a new baby sister. Every day she helped Mummy to look after her. She fetched the nappies or the baby powder when her Mummy needed them and rocked the pram when baby Anne cried.

Today was a very important day. Mummy and Daddy were taking baby Anne to the church to be baptised. Helen had helped her Mummy to wash and dress baby Anne quite early and now while Mummy and Daddy were getting ready she talked to the baby as she lay in her pram.

"We are all going to the church today," Helen told her. "You and Mummy and Daddy and me." Baby Anne smiled, but she was far too small to understand what Helen was saying to her.

On the way to the church Helen asked, "Why does the minister baptise little babies? Anne won't know anything about it, will she?"

"No," said Daddy, "but even though Anne isn't big enough yet to know anything about her baptism *we* are remembering that she belongs not only to our family but to the Church family too."

In the church, Helen sat by her Mummy and Daddy right next to the font. After the hymn, Daddy took baby Anne very gently in his arms and gave her to the minister.

Then the minister put his hand into the water in the font and as he sprinkled a little of the water on the baby's head he said, "Anne, I baptise you in the name of the Father, and of the Son, and of the Holy Spirit. Amen."

"Anne belongs to our church family," he said. "And we must help to look after her as she grows up in the church."

ACTIVITIES

(i) A portrait gallery. The main activity this week might be for all the children and teachers to draw or paint a picture of themselves on a large sheet of paper and write their names underneath. These could be hung up in class groups around the room. If the teacher is reluctant to draw a picture of herself then some children could paint one of her and she could write a sentence about herself to complete the portrait gallery. A large strip of paper across the top of

each group of pictures could say, "Our Sunday school class"; or "We all come to ———— church."

(ii) Modelling. The children could make figures from newspaper rolls or pipe-cleaners to represent "their class." These could be dressed in pieces of brightly coloured scrap materials.

(iii) The group scrapbook. Pictures and writing about "Our Sunday school class" could be incorporated.

(iv) Game. The children might sing and act out. "This is the way we go to church . . ." to the tune, "Mulberry Bush."

(v) Use can be made of the worksheets.

2 Thanking God for the world he has given us

PREPARING FOR THIS THEME

This theme is designed for use at the time of the harvest festival which in most cases will take place during October. The theme need not be used in the order presented here, but the talk on harvest thanksgiving should coincide with the local festival.

TIME OF YEAR

Thanksgiving is a very important part of the harvest festival. Adults probably appreciate the fact that thanksgiving is offered for all the fruits of the earth which they enjoy but this must be demonstrated to the children, as this theme attempts to do. Thanksgiving for our food is perhaps uppermost in our minds at harvest but the earth yields many more things for our use. Among them are minerals, gas, and other sources of power as well as materials for clothing. This theme attempts to include these aspects in the thanksgiving which the children offer at harvest.

APPROACH TO THEME

Read Deut. 10: 14. Here is a strong statement that "the earth with all that is in it" belongs to the Lord. Used in the right way these gifts to men can bring great benefits.

BIBLICAL FOUNDATIONS

In Ps. 24: 1 the writer asserts "The earth is the Lord's and the fulness thereof: the world and those who dwell therein."

This idea is further developed in the New Testament, where Jesus is seen as God's agent: the same love which meets us in him is responsible for the whole creation. "He was in the beginning with God; all things were made through him, and without him was not anything made that was made." (John 1 : 2-3.)

"For in him all things were created in heaven and on earth, visible and invisible . . . all things were created through him and for him." (Col. 1 : 16.)

"The earth belongs unto the Lord"

Thanks to the discoveries of modern science we have a fuller knowledge than the men of the Old Testament had of what the earth contains. The powers that can be realised from it for the use of man exceed anything that the ancient world dreamt of; gas, electricity, atomic energy. Because of the tremendous potential which these powers hold it is more than ever necessary that they should be used for the good of mankind. If they are wrongly used they can bring devastation and destruction.

The harvest festival gives an opportunity to the church to emphasise that the earth belongs to the Lord. The children can learn to think of all the modern wonders as gifts from God, and to offer thanks for them and for those whose work harnesses the powers for our use. Upon this foundation a fuller understanding can be built in later years—the idea of using these gifts in God's way.

The harvest festival

PRIMARY WORSHIP

Suitable hymns for this theme might be—"All things bright and beautiful" (I.P. 1) ; "For the beauty of the earth" (I.P. 4 : 1) ; "Thank you for the world so sweet" (I.P. 41) ; "God who made the earth" (R.C.H. 20 : 1-4) ; "We plough the fields and scatter" (R.C.H. 618 : 1 and chorus).

The Bible reading for the second week might be introduced in the following way. "Before we say thank you to God for our food, our clothes and the houses we live in, let us listen to this verse from the Bible about the things God has given us." Read Psalm 104 : 24.

Other suitable Bible readings : Gen. 8 : 22 ; Ps. 24 : 1 ; Col. 1 : 16a.

In the third week the prayer of thanksgiving should include the men who provide us with whichever source of power is chosen.

THE THEME IN OUTLINE

First week: "Thanking God for our food."

A brief informal talk introduces a filmstrip on providers of food which explains how we obtain milk for our daily food. The appropriate frames of the filmstrip (Nos. 17-24) conclude with a prayer of thanksgiving.

Second week: "Thanking God for our clothes and houses."

This follows the pattern of the previous week, using the filmstrip (Frames 25-32) dealing with our clothes and houses

Third week: "Thanking God for things that heat our houses."

This material encourages the children to think of the sources of power and heat as gifts of God. A choice of four short stories is offered to teachers. They deal respectively with coal, electricity, gas and peat. No more than two should be used. At the close of the week's work the children should be encouraged to make up their prayer of thanks for things that heat their homes.

Fourth week: "Harvest thanksgiving."

The children will spend rather longer in church this week but a short story is included telling of the harvest thanksgiving in Santalia, India.

Suggestions for the Book Corner

The Farm; The Farmer; The Miner; Public Services—Gas; Public Services— Electricity. (Ladybird.)

"Our Book Corner" series—*The Sheep; Milk, Butter and Cheese; Bread.* (W. & R. Chambers Ltd.)

I.T.A. "Read about it" series by O. B. Gregory. (1) *Bread;* (2) *Milk;* (7) *Sheep Farmers;* (9) *Coal Miners.* (A. Wheaton & Co. Ltd., Exeter.)

FOR THE TEACHER

Useful leaflets and information for this theme can be obtained from the following addresses :

British Wool Marketing Board, Oak Mills, Clayton, Bradford, Yorks.

Scottish Milk Publicity Council Ltd., 41 St. Vincent Place, Glasgow, C.1.

McDougalls Ltd., Wheatsheaf Mills, London, E.14.

Flour Advisory Bureau, 21 Arlington Street, London, S.W.1.

National Coal Board, Public Relations Department, Hobart House, London, S.W.1.

Electricity Council, Marketing Division, Trafalgar Buildings, 1 Charing Cross, London, S.W.1.

Gas Council, 59 Bryanston Street, London, W.1.

Local electricity, coal and gas showrooms may also have useful pictures for this theme.

Material on peat may be obtained from guide books, such as "The Shetland Isles Guide Book" obtainable from the Scottish Tourist Board, Ravelston Terrace, Edinburgh, or the Highlands and Islands Board, Inverness.

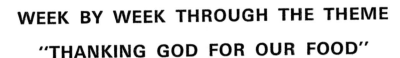

WEEK BY WEEK THROUGH THE THEME

"THANKING GOD FOR OUR FOOD"

FIRST WEEK

BOTH SECTIONS

INFORMAL TALK

Ask the children what their favourite food is. What do they like best for dinner, or tea? What is their favourite drink? Why do they like these?

If someone had nothing to eat or drink and was starving, what kind of food would be best for him? (*Milk.*) *Let the children look at some powdered milk.*

Explain that milk is one of the best foods there is. When the crops in Africa and India fail and the children have nothing to eat or drink, milk is one of the first things that is sent to them. In our country, too, we drink milk at school, because it helps us to be strong and healthy.

Today, we will watch a filmstrip which will tell us about how we get our milk.

FILMSTRIP

The filmstrip, "People Show God's Love," can be obtained from Religious Films Ltd., 6 Eaton Gate, London, S.W.1, who also supplied the commentary printed below. The frames used today are numbers 17 to 24. The earlier frames were used in Themes 1 and 5 of *Growing Up in the Church—Second Year*.

Frame 17—"Oh! Good! This is the day we are going to visit the farm with our teacher," said Peter. "We are going to find out how we get some of our food."

Frame 18—The children went on a coach to the farm, with pencils and note-books in their pockets. There were many cows in the milking shed. The farmer explained how the cows were milked by machine. "It's much better than hand milking," he said.

Frame 19—The bottling factory was just as interesting ; one machine washed and sterilised[1] the bottles, another machine filled them with milk, and the metal tops were put on by a third machine. "Look how clean it is," said the teacher. "All the men wear white overalls and caps."

Frame 20—At tea-time, Peter had lots of things to tell the family ; it had been a marvellous day. "How do we get our bread ?" he asked, as he ate a mouthful. Father replied, "Wait until I hang my coat and then we'll see what we can find out about the wheat which is used for bread and cakes and biscuits."

Frame 21—"Remember the shopping we did on Monday," said Mother. "In the supermarket we got buns and bread. They had been made in a factory from flour and yeast."

Frame 22—Father got out the children's encyclopaedia. "Here is a picture of a combine harvester on a Canadian farm," he said. "Most of the wheat used for making our bread is grown in Canada. They have plenty of sun to ripen the wheat."

Frame 23—"I remember that holiday we had in the country," said Peter. "When it rained and rained. The farmer said that the rain was just right for his wheat," said Father. Jane looked at all the things on the tea-table. "Think of all the people who help to provide our tea," she said.

Frame 24—Thank you, God, for all the food we enjoy.
Thank you, God, for the farmers whose cows supply us with milk.
Thank you, God, for the farmers who send eggs and wheat from other countries.
Thank you, God, for sailors and dockers who make sure we get our food.
Thank you, for mothers who shop and cook for us.
Help us to remember those who are hungry.

ACTIVITIES

(i) Drawing and painting. The children might draw, paint or make a frieze of a farm and farm animals, especially cows. The frieze might show the story of milk as presented on the filmstrip.

(ii) Modelling. A farmyard scene with buildings. fields, hedges, trees, animals, carts, tractors, present a good opportunity for modelling. Clay or plasticine may be used for figures and animals, paper or towelling material for the fields cardboard for the buildings and tractor.

(iii) Writing. The older children, particularly, could write about a visit to the farm or the story of milk.

(iv) Poster. Teachers might try to collect pictures from newspapers and magazines showing milk being given to people in areas of need. The children could cut some of them out and paste them on a poster.

[1] Teacher should explain that this kills the germs.

(v) Scrapbook. Some children might make a scrapbook of the harvest or "Thanking God for His Gifts." It should include any pictures cut out as indicated above and also their own drawings and writing about milk or farms.

(vi) Wonder table. This should be given a prominent place during this theme. A bottle of milk, some powdered milk, bread, biscuits, ears of corn might be included today. Encourage the children to bring things for this table.

(vii) Worksheets may be used as an additional activity.

"THANKING GOD FOR OUR CLOTHES AND HOUSES"

SECOND WEEK

Ask the children to imagine that they are getting ready to go to school on a cold morning. They have had their breakfast and got their schoolbag ready. What do they put on before they go out into the cold? (*Coat, scarf, gloves.*)

BOTH SECTIONS
INFORMAL TALK

We need clothes to keep us warm and to keep out the rain and the cold. Can you think of any people who wear special clothes to keep them warm or dry? (*Fishermen, roadmen, policemen.*)

Do you know that some people have to wear clothes to protect themselves from the sun? Do you know of any? (*People who live in hot countries cover their heads; Jews and Arabs.* Jesus would do so, too, for he lived in a hot country.)

Clothes are important. When some terrible accident has happened, like an earthquake, and people's homes and all they have are destroyed, we send them clothes and blankets. We send money, too, to help to build houses for them.
Clothes and houses! Let's think about the people who provide us with them.

The pictures in the filmstrip tell us something about them. (Frames 25-32 of "People Show God's Love" should be used this Sunday.)

FILMSTRIP

Frame 25—"Peter had to find out about food," said Jane. "Our class is thinking about the clothes we wear and the homes in which we live."

Frame 26—One day Peter and Jane went to see Grandmother. "Look what I have knitted for you, Peter," said Grandmother. She held out a new pullover. "Thank you," said Peter. "I shall be able to wear it at school this winter."

Frame 27—"Now I can start a cardigan for Jane," said Grandmother. "I have bought some orange wool to match your party dress, Jane, but I need you to help me to wind the wool."

Peter picked up a book. "This is an interesting book; it's all about the houses we live in."

Frame 28—"Can I make something?" asked Jane. Grandmother got out some bits of material. "What about making a dress for your doll?" she said. Carefully, Jane cut out a dress. "What is this material made of?" asked Jane. Grandmother told her it was woollen material. "Where does the wool come from?"

Frame 29—Peter rushed to the bookcase. "Have you got a picture of sheep-shearing in Australia?" he asked Grandmother.

"The men have an electric machine and they can each shear over one hundred sheep in a day. Then the wool is sold in great bales, ready to be spun and woven into cloth."

Frame 30—"I know," said Jane. "We have a picture on the wall at school which shows a weaving loom in a factory. I am going to do some weaving when I get some wool. I want to make a scarf for my doll."

Frame 31—Grandmother took the children to the shops, so that Jane could buy some wool. Peter saw a collecting box on the counter. "Homeless refugees," he read. "Look, Grandmother! We have lovely houses in Scotland, but lots of people have nowhere to live. Can I put some money in the box to help the refugees?" Grandmother watched while Peter put some of his pocket money in the box. Jane put the change from the price of her wool. "We are lucky to have a home; we want to help other people."

Frame 32—"Thank you, God, for our clothes, for the sheep-shearers of Australia and the weavers in the factories.

"Thank you, God, for our homes, for the bricklayers and plumbers who build our houses. Help us to care about refugees who have no homes."

ACTIVITIES

(i) Continue drawing and modelling as for previous week, paying particular attention to sheep and the story of wool.

(ii) A further modelling project might include dressing dolls, especially with woollen clothes. Alternatively, newspaper or clothes-peg figures might be made and dressed. (See *Growing Up in the Church—First Year*, p. 28.) The

purpose of this activity is to draw attention to different materials of clothing and in particular to distinguish wool from the others. The teacher could also discuss with the children the kind of material from which their own clothes are made.

(iii) Collage. A large collage picture may be made showing sheep in their natural surroundings. Almost all kinds of material can be incorporated, but it would be particularly useful to have scraps of wool to represent the sheep.

(iv) A poster showing the various textures of materials might also be made by a group of children.

(v) The scrapbook should be continued incorporating pictures of sheep being shorn, and various kinds of woollen material.

(vi) Wonder table. If any of the children have a small weaving loom they might be encouraged to bring this along for the "Wonder Table" which should also have sheep's wool on it today. The various kinds of knitting, a knitted garment and pieces of woollen material might also be included.

(vii) Use can be made of the worksheet.

"THANKING GOD FOR THE THINGS THAT HEAT OUR HOUSES"

THIRD WEEK

Note for teachers

Teachers should begin by discussing with the children the things that heat their houses: e.g., gas, electricity, coal or peat. Then select *one* of the stories given below. Obviously, it should be the one most of the children know best. When the story has been told, say, "But some children in Scotland have houses that are heated in a different way . . ." and introduce an unusual story. For instance, children in the Lowlands of Scotland might be told about peat, which will be familiar to most children in the north and in the isles. Before the children leave their class group they should make up a prayer of the same kind as on the filmstrip, thanking God for the things that heat their homes and for the people whose job it is to bring it to their houses.

DISCUSSION WITH THE CHILDREN

Ask the children what keeps their houses warm. Is it a coal fire, or a gas fire, or electricity or central heating? Do they like to sit near it? What does it feel like to come in to your house when the fire's not on?

Then say, "Most of you seem to have gas fires (or 'coal' or 'electric') in your houses. Do you know where it comes from?"

"THE STORY OF COAL"

Who brings the coal to your house? (*The coalman.*) But where does the coalman get it from? He gets it from the coal pit. He may take his lorry to the coal pit and fill it with coal, or the coal may be brought to him in railway wagons. In his yard or in the railway yard, the coalman fills his bags with coal and brings it to your house.

(*Look at picture in the Ladybird book, "The Miner."*)

But who gets the coal for him at the coal pit? Who digs it out of the ground? (*The miner.*) Each day, the miners go into the big lift that takes them down below the ground. Then they sometimes have a long way to walk in the tunnels under the ground to reach the place where they are digging coal, but sometimes there is a little train that carries them along the tunnel. Long ago, it used to be very dark in the coal mine, and the men were only able to see by the light of the lamp on their cap. But now many mines are well lit, and the men can see where they are going. Long ago, too, the miners had to dig the coal out of the ground with picks and shovels, and sometimes they had to lie on their backs to get to it. Now they have machines which cut it for them. Machines also carry the coal back along the tunnels and separate the stones from the good coal. At last it is ready to be sent to your coalman, who will bring it to your house.

What happens to your hands if you carry a piece of coal in them? (*They become dirty.*) The miner, too, gets dirty when he is working with the coal, but nowadays there are big baths at the pit where he can wash all the coal dust off before he goes home.

"THE STORY OF ELECTRICITY"

If you have electric fires in your house, do you know how Mummy or Daddy puts them on or off? Yes. There is a switch, just like the switch for the electric light. When the switch is turned on, it lets the electricity into the fire and the fire heats up.

The electricity is carried into the house by wires which are in the wall. If something goes wrong and there is a breakdown, Mummy or Daddy sends for a man to fix it. Do you know what he is called? (*An electrician.*)

But the electrician does not make electricity. He just fixes the wires. The electricity is made in big power stations, where there is a lot of machinery. Sometimes coal is used to drive these big machines and sometimes water is used. If water is used, there will be a big dam or loch near the power station.

After the electricity is made, it is carried across the countryside in huge wires, held up in the air by big metal posts called pylons. Maybe some of you have seen them. It can also be carried in cables under the ground. At last, it is brought into our houses, and when you press the switch, on it comes to heat our homes or give light or perhaps to cook our meals.

(*Look at pictures in the Ladybird book, "Electricity."*)

"THE STORY OF GAS"   *THIRD STORY*

Many of you have gas fires in your houses. Perhaps Mummy uses gas, too, to cook your meals and to heat her oven when she bakes. How does the gas come into your house? Do any of you know?

Gas comes into your house through a pipe. Where does the pipe come from? It comes from the gas works, where the gas is made. Do you know how it is made?

Gas is sometimes made from coal. If you have ever watched coal burning in the fire, you will have seen the tiny little blue and green and yellow flames that sometimes burn on the outside of the lumps of coal. That is the gas that comes from the coal when it is heated: "coal gas" it is called. And in the gas works, the gas is taken out of the coal and made ready to be piped to your house.

(*Look at pictures in the Ladybird book, "Gas."*)

But there are other ways of getting gas. Men work out in the North Sea on oil-rigs. These are funny looking towers which seem to float on the water but have long legs which reach right down to the bottom of the sea. The oil-rig has a big drill which bored deep down into the earth below the sea. And what do you think it struck? Gas! This is called "natural gas," and this gas is now being brought in pipes underneath the sea to our country where it is made ready for us to use in our houses. (Look at the photograph facing p. 33.)

"THE STORY OF PEAT"   *FOURTH STORY*

Have you heard of a peat fire? Some boys and girls in Scotland know what peat is, for they have a stack of it outside the door of their house, and a big piece of peat may be burning on the kitchen fire just now.

At the beginning of the summer the whole family go out to the moors. The men and sometimes the women, too, shovel aside the top soil until they un-cover the rich black peat. Then the men take a special kind of spade, called a tuskar. It has a very sharp blade to cut the peat, and a bent part, called the heel, which helps them to cut the peat evenly and it is then put on to the heather to dry. The women and children work hard during the summer, turning it over until it is completely dried. Then comes the big job of carrying it home. Sometimes it is put in baskets which are pulled along a wire until they reach the road, where the peat can be loaded on to lorries or carts. It is stacked in a big heap outside the house ready to be used when summer has passed. (Look at the photograph facing p. 33.)

Peat is very hot when it burns, so that it is good for heating the room and also for cooking on the stove. As the peat burns, the room is filled with its pleasant smell. Many years ago, the people who lived in the mountains of Scotland and in the islands had no electricity or any other way to heat their houses. But even today many people still use peat and are very thankful for its heat in the cold winter nights.

ACTIVITIES   (i) Drawing and painting. The children might draw or paint a room in their house showing how it is heated, or they might draw a picture of the story they have heard.

(ii) Model. If the talk has been about electricity, the children might make a model of a line of pylons. These could be incorporated in the farmyard scene made two weeks ago.

(iii) Poster or frieze. A large poster or frieze showing the four methods of heat can be made.

(iv) Scrapbook. The children's drawings, writing and prayers they have made up themselves about heating can be included. Pictures of miners, people cutting peat, etc., can also be incorporated.

(v) Wonder table. This week there should be pieces of coal and if possible. peat, on the table.

(vi) Use can be made of the worksheets.

FOURTH WEEK   # HARVEST THANKSGIVING

Some of the models and posters made by the children during this theme might be displayed in the church on harvest thanksgiving Sunday.

Note to teachers   It is assumed that on harvest thanksgiving Sunday the children will be in church for longer than usual and that the time spent in Sunday school will be brief. It is also taken for granted that the children will be involved in bringing gifts for the harvest service, and, if possible, in distributing some of them with an adult.

It should be remembered that we celebrate the harvest in a land of plenty, and that others are not so fortunate. Accordingly, the theme of Christian Aid should be associated with the harvest gifts and perhaps be a special Sunday school project this month.

BOTH SECTIONS   Ask the children what special service is being held in church today. Discuss
INFORMAL TALK what happens in church today ; What do people do ? What gifts do they bring ? (Let the children describe in detail.) What is done with the gifts afterwards. and why is this done ?

STORY   We hold our harvest thanksgiving in the autumn, when the harvest in the fields is ready to be gathered in. But if we lived in a very warm country, like Santalia in India, we might hold our harvest service in January.

On harvest Sunday there, the people gather outside their white-washed church in the bright morning sunshine. The bell is rung three times, and then the men and women, with the boys and girls, walk round the outside of the church singing a Santal harvest hymn to the tune of "We plough the fields and scatter"—a hymn that we will sing ourselves today. As they walk round their church, the women carry big baskets on their heads, and these baskets are filled with rice and vegetables, their gift for their harvest thanksgiving.

The women wear their bright coloured saris, their long Indian dresses. The men wear white shirts and shorts, and the children wear the new clothes they received at Christmas time.

After their procession round the church, they enter the building and each one walks forward and lays a gift on the steps in front of the Communion table. Many of them are poor people, but they give willingly of what they have.

Then the service begins. The windows of the church are wide open. The birds are singing outside, and butterflies fly in and out as the hymns begin and the people thank God for all his gifts.

ACTIVITIES

This week the children might help to distribute the harvest gifts. It would also be possible for them to make cards to convey the best wishes of the Sunday school to the people to whom they are being sent.

If Christian Aid or a similar project is incorporated in this theme, the Sunday school might make an effort to raise money for Christian Aid so that milk could be supplied for children in need in other lands. The Red Cross often welcome gifts of clothing and blankets and this would be another useful project to mount.

3 The people of our Church

PREPARING FOR THIS THEME

TIME OF YEAR

This theme does not reflect any seasonal interest and could be used at any time of year. In this programme it is suggested for November.

APPROACH TO THEME

When Primary children think of the Church they think most readily of their own local church, the place to which they come on a Sunday morning. But the Church is more than this; it is the people.

This theme begins by drawing the children's attention to the people who come to their church, old and young, and encourages them to feel part of this family. It aims at helping them to discover that the people of the Church are "real" people who serve God not only on Sunday inside the church building but every day as they live and witness in the world.

BIBLICAL FOUNDATIONS

The Church is people

The Church is a company of people called by God to his service. They serve him not only as they worship in a building but as they respond to the love of Christ in their daily life. They are united to each other by Christ even though they differ in race, temperament, ideas or achievement.

The first disciples show a great variety of outlook and character, but are united as followers of Jesus.

Read John 1: 35-51; Luke 5: 27. Who else could unite people as different as Levi (a tax-gatherer regarded by many as a quisling) and Nathaniel (a zealous nationalist)? Each is valued for his own gifts; all benefit from the contribution of each individual.

The Body of Christ

Read 1 Cor. 12: 12-27. St. Paul speaks of the Church as "the body of Christ." Each part of the body carries out its own function, and health of the body depends upon the effective working of each part. Action is determined by the head, which for the Church is Christ. (*See Rom. 12: 3-8; Eph. 4: 15; Eph. 1: 23.*)

Christ's purposes are to be worked out by the living Church. His love is unchanging. He fed the hungry; healed the sick; released lives that were imprisoned by superstition and ignorance; and the Church must continue to do this.

A practical faith

Read Eph. 4: 1-16. We need to find our place within the body of Christ, to use our capabilities honestly and without envy or disparagement of the gifts of others.

We shall be thinking during this theme of various ways in which people are using their gifts as followers of Jesus. These are not the only ways, but they illustrate a call to very different people to be channels through which the love of Christ reaches others. The Church exists for the sake of others as Jesus lived for others. Whatever our gifts he invites us to use them fully.

A wedding in church.

An elder calls on a family in his district.

(Home Board photographs)

Ministers meet
people everywhere.

One of the many duties of the church officer.

(Home Board photographs)

PRIMARY WORSHIP

A suitable song for the theme is "God, we thank you" (p. 164).

Other appropriate hymns and songs are "At Church" (p. 159) ; "The Church is wherever God's people are praising" (S.H.P.C. 142) ; "Children, come!" (p. 163) ; "Sing a glad song" (I.P. 38).

To introduce the Bible reading for the first week the leader might say, "I'm going to read a verse from the Bible that was written a long time ago by a man who was glad when he went to church." Read Ps. 122: 1. Other Bible readings might include Ps. 100: 4 ; 1 Cor. 3: 9 ; James 1: 22.

THE THEME IN OUTLINE

First week: "The people who come to our church."

The theme begins by encouraging the children to talk about their church and the people they see there.

Second week: "The minister of our church."

The story of Neil and Iain spending a day with their minister introduces the children to the work of their minister.

Third week: "We meet the people of our church."

This week the children meet some of the people of the church and discover various ways in which they use their gifts as followers of Jesus.

Fourth week: "The people of our church are helpers."

The children are now given the opportunity of becoming involved in helping in their own church.

Suggestions for the Book Corner

The Bus that Went to Church (Faber).

A book might be made using photographs of your own church.

WEEK BY WEEK THROUGH THE THEME

"THE PEOPLE WHO COME TO OUR CHURCH"

FIRST WEEK

BOTH SECTIONS

INFORMAL TALK

Encourage the children to talk about the people who come to their church.

Ask who came with them to the church this morning. (*Mummy, Daddy, Granny, big sister, friends.*)

Ask if they saw other people coming to church.

The teacher could say: "On my way to church I saw Mr. McNeil, the grocer, with his family. Mr. McNeil is an elder in our church ; he gave me a hymn-book when I came into the church."

c

Encourage the children to join in, "On my way to church I saw . . ."

Now ask the children who they saw in the church this morning. Who carried in the Bible? Who played the organ? Who sang in the choir?

Mention the minister's name and what he does in the church.

Ask the children what we do in our church. (*We sing, we pray, we listen to someone reading from the Bible.*)

Remind the children that sometimes babies come to our church. Why do they come? (*To be baptised.*)

Point out that the babies are too small to come to the church every Sunday (unless there is a creche) but when they are bigger they will come to church, too.

Point out that many people come to our church, ourselves, our friends, other boys and girls, Mummies and Daddies and other grown-up people, too.

ACTIVITIES

The children might choose from the following activities:

(i) A project. One project which can be continued throughout this theme is to make a new *table cloth* for the worship centre. Choose a brightly coloured material for the background. The children could decorate it by glueing or sewing on scraps of coloured felt to represent the seasons, e.g., cut out autumn coloured leaves for one corner; spring flowers for another; let the children make their own suggestions for the design. (For further projects, see p. 74.)

(ii) Painting or collage. A group of children could make a frieze "The people who come to our church." This could be a picture of their own church with themselves and other people coming to the church. Encourage the children to write a caption under their picture.

(iii) A model. A simple model could be made from the children's own drawings. Let the children paint or crayon figures of people on to card and cut them out. A piece of card 6" x ½" fixed into a circle with a staple makes a stand for the figures. Fix the figure to the stand with two staples. A background of the church could be painted for the model.

(iv) A book for the Book Corner. Let the children draw pictures or write about some of the people they have been talking about in the informal talk. The book could include a picture of the church, a baptism, the church officer carrying in the Bible, people at worship.

(v) Dramatisation. Provide a few simple props such as handbags, dolls, a clerical collar, a piece of material to suggest a gown. A group of children might like to dramatise the church service and this could include a baptism. It is important that the children make their own suggestions. The teacher should guide the suggestions made by the children rather than direct the dramatisation.

(vi) A poster. Some children might like to make a poster about "The people who come to church." This could be made in the same way as the scrapbook, but the children's drawings and writing might be glued on to a large sheet of paper and displayed as a poster.

(vii) The worksheets can be used as an alternative activity.

"THE MINISTER OF OUR CHURCH"

SECOND WEEK

Note to teachers

If it is possible, arrangements should be made for the minister to visit the Primary for a short time this Sunday or alternatively the children could meet him in the vestry after the morning service.

BOTH SECTIONS
Introduction

Ask the children if they know the name of their minister. Ask what he did in the church this morning. Ask if they know what he does during the week. Encourage them to tell of his visits to people they know.

STORY

It was the holidays and Iain and Neil were playing in the tent in Neil's garden.

"I know your Dad's a minister," said Iain, "and he preaches in our church every Sunday, but what does he do during the week?"

Just then Neil's Daddy came outside.

"Time for bed," he called. "Pack up your tent and say goodnight."

"But Daddy," said Neil, "Iain wants to know what you do during the week. Will you tell him?"

"It's rather late tonight," said Mr. Stewart, "but if you come round early tomorrow, Iain, you can spend the whole day with Neil and I'll show both of you some of the things I do."

"Oh, thank you," said Iain. "I'll be there," and off he ran.

Early next morning Iain was at the manse door. (*Teachers could explain that the minister's house is called a manse.*)

"Come in," called Mr. Stewart, and Iain and Neil both went into Mr. Stewart's study.

"I spend almost every morning in my study," said Mr. Stewart. "I read some books and write letters and prepare my sermon ready for the service on Sunday. Today I must read some of this book, so you can either read a book, too, or find a quiet game to play."

Iain looked around the room. He'd never seen so many books before. "Did Neil's Daddy read all these?" he wondered.

Before long the telephone rang. "Mrs. Morris is in hospital, Ward 11. Would the minister visit her, please?"

"Yes, I'm going to visit a number of people who are ill in hospital this afternoon," said Mr. Stewart. "I'll call and see Mrs. Morris."

Next, the door bell rang. It was Mrs. Shaw with her pension book for the minister to sign.

"Did you know that Mr. Wallace is ill again?" she enquired. "No, I didn't," said Mr. Stewart, "but thanks for letting me know. I'll call and see him this evening after the vestry hour."

Mr. Stewart only had time to read a little more of his book before lunch was ready. Neil and Iain ate their lunch quickly and went outside to play. Before they had been in the garden long enough to put up their tent again, Mr. Stewart was calling them.

"I must be off to visit some people who are in hospital now," he said. "I have to be back to take a wedding service at half past three. Are you coming with me?"

"Yes, wait for us," they shouted.

"Jump in the car, then," said Mr. Stewart, and off they went to the hospital.

At the hospital Neil and Iain were not allowed into the wards with Mr. Stewart but as they waited in the corridors there were many things for them to see. Doctors and nurses were hurrying along the corridor, some patients went by on trolleys to the X-ray room, ambulances were arriving outside with new patients. It was an interesting afternoon.

Mr. Stewart visited Mrs. Morris and all the other people from the church who were patients at the hospital and now he had to hurry back to the church for the wedding.

Back at the church, the church officer had opened the big front doors and the wedding guests were arriving.

"You can go up into the gallery to watch the wedding," said Mr. Stewart. "You should have a good view from there. I must go into the vestry to change into my robes."

Neil and Iain crept quietly up the big stone steps into the gallery to watch the wedding service. Mr. Stewart was right, they did have a good view. Iain thought the bride looked super in her long white dress.

After the wedding service was over, Neil and Iain went to the vestry to see Mr. Stewart.

"I have to go to the party after the wedding now," he said. "I hope you have enjoyed your day."

"Yes, we have," said Iain and Neil together. "Thanks for taking us with you."

"What a lot of different things your Dad does!" said Iain on the way home for tea.

ACTIVITIES

The children might choose from the following activities:

(i) The project should be continued.

(ii) Painting or collage. A group of children might make a frieze showing various aspects of the minister's work; preaching, visiting in homes and hospitals, a wedding. Let the children write captions under their pictures.

(iii) Modelling. Using newspaper or clothes-peg figures the children could make a model depicting some of the work of the minister. Provide pieces of lace and satin material to suggest a wedding scene. A large cardboard carton might suggest a hospital ward, matchbox trays, with headboards cut from cardboard and glued on, make beds. The children could make the bed-clothes from scraps of material and the patients from plasticine or dough.

(iv) A book for the Book Corner. This week pictures and writing telling of the work of the minister can be added.

(v) Dramatisation. Pieces of lace curtains, a clerical collar, a doctor or nurse set, a telephone, cups and saucers can be added to the dressing-up box this week. The children might play out various scenes of the minister's work. A wedding and a hospital scene will probably appeal to the children.

(vi) A poster. With the drawings and writings the children have done, a poster could be made showing the various aspects of the minister's work.

(vii) The worksheets can be used as an alternative activity.

"WE MEET THE PEOPLE OF OUR CHURCH"

THIRD WEEK

Note to Teachers

At the preparation class try to arrange for at least two people of the church to visit the Primary this week. One person can meet the older section and the other the younger section. If more people are willing to help in this way, smaller groups could be arranged, making a much more informal atmosphere in the department.

Arrangements must be made well in advance for this week. The people who have been asked to share in this theme must know exactly what is required of them and be sympathetic to the present approach in the Sunday school. The Primary leader and some of the teachers should meet with the people before the theme begins, perhaps inviting them to the preparation class when this theme is discussed. In the notes which follow, an elder who may be the Session Clerk and the Church Treasurer are given as examples of people who could meet with the older section, the church officer and flower convener for the younger section. Other visitors might be the Sunday school superintendent or leader of another department, a member of the choir, the Boys' Brigade captain, a deaconess, a day school teacher, doctor, nurse or missionary who may be a member of the church.

The children cannot take in information about several people at one session but this plan could be followed on more than one Sunday if people are willing to help.

SUGGESTED MATERIAL FOR THE TALKS

**YOUNGER
SECTION**

(Teachers should stay with their class groups and help to guide the discussion.)

The visitors could introduce themselves to their particular group of children by telling them their names, something about their families and the work they do during the week.

**The Church
Officer**

Ask the children if they saw the church officer in the church this morning. What does he do in the service? (*Carries in the Bible.*)

The church officer could tell the children that he rang the bell before the service began. Ask the children if they heard it ringing. Why does he ring it? (*It tells the people of the church that it's nearly time for the service to begin.*)

What other things does the church officer do? The church officer could explain that he keeps the church warm and clean, ready for the service on Sunday. He could mention other people who help him with this work. He could tell the children how he uses a big brush for sweeping the floor, dusters for dusting the pulpit, Communion table and pews, polish for the brass vases for the flowers.

He might explain that sometimes he puts water in the font. Why does he do this? (*For the minister to baptise the babies.*)

When there is a wedding in the church, what does he do? (*Opens the church doors; sometimes he rings the bell.*)

If the church has grounds around it, he could tell how he cuts the grass and weeds the garden and paths.

After the morning service the church officer should show this group around the church building, pointing out the pulpit, Communion table, font, lectern and pews. He might also show them where he keeps his brushes and polish for cleaning the church and where he goes to ring the bell.

**The Flower
Convener**

Ask the children if they saw the flowers in the church this morning. Where were they? Who put them there? Explain to the children that every Sunday someone gives flowers to make the church look more beautiful. The flower convener could explain that before the service begins the flowers have to be arranged in the big vases.

Ask the children who arranged the flowers.

Ask them if they know what happens to the flowers when the services are over. The flower convener could explain that they are taken to sick people or old people in the community. Point out that by doing this the people of the church are showing that they care for these people as Jesus cared for others.

At this point she could show the group some of the cards that are taken out with the flowers each week.

After the morning service the flower convener should take this group of children into the church to look at the flowers. If possible she should take a few of the children with her to distribute some flowers (possibly those from the Primary worship centre) to a person who is sick or old.

Ask the children if they know any of the elders in their church. (Perhaps they will know the name of the elder who visits their house.)

Tell the children that the elders in the church help the minister in his work and see that the work of the church is carried out. They visit people in their homes, care for the sick and lonely in the district.

At this point the elder should tell the children of any interesting visits he has made recently.

He should point out that the elders also help the minister with the Communion service.

Ask the children if they know the name of the table in their church. (*The Communion table.*)

What does it look like? Where does it stand? Ask if they know what it is used for. (They may have noticed the flowers, a cross or a Bible on it.)

Tell the children that sometimes the church looks different. Explain that on Communion Sundays, the Communion table is prepared with a white table cloth, and that at the service the minister and elders sit round the table. Ask the children if they know what this service is called. (*The Communion service.*) Tell how the elders help to take the bread and wine to the congregation. If the elders help the minister to take the Communion to the homes of people who are too ill or too elderly to come to the church, tell the children of this.

The elder should show the Communion cards that he takes out to the people to remind them of the Communion service; he might also show the Communion cups and plates.

After the morning service the children should visit the church with the elder to have a closer look at the Communion table. If it is possible this group might visit the church on Communion Sunday to see the Communion table and pews before the service begins.

Remind the children of the offerings they bring to the church each Sunday. The Church Treasurer should explain that all the people of the church bring their offerings too. Ask the children if they have seen the large plate on the Communion table. Ask them if they know what it is used for.

At this point the treasurer should show the children the offering bags or plates and explain how they are used in the church. He could also show the offering envelopes and tell how they are used.

Ask the children if they know what happens to the offerings that the people bring to the church.

Explain that some of the gifts are used for heating and lighting the church; to build new churches in new towns and some to send missionaries to other countries so that the people there can hear the good news of Jesus.

Arrange for the children in this group to go with the Church Treasurer into the church to see the offering being uplifted by the office-bearers and received by the minister.

At the preparation class the teachers should prepare a poster for the children to look at, using pictures cut from the popular reports published annually by the Overseas Council, Home Board and the Committee on Social Service.

Copies of these reports, at a small charge, can be purchased from the respective departments, 121 George Street, Edinburgh, EH2 4YN.

ACTIVITIES

(i) The project should be continued.

(ii) Painting or collage. Various scenes could be made either by painting or collage showing the work that is done by those who visited the Primary today. This could be a group frieze or individual work. (See photograph, facing p. 32.)

(iii) A group of children could arrange the flowers for the worship centre. The flower convener might help with this. Perhaps a real flower arrangement could be attempted, using an "Oasis" and bowl. The flowers could then be taken to someone who is sick or elderly with a card of greeting from the Sunday school.

(iv) A book for the Book Corner. This week pictures of the people who visited the department and writing telling of the work they do in the church can be added.

(v) Dramatisation. A clerical collar, long dresses, handbags, pieces of material could be added to the dressing-up box this week. The children might like to dramatise the church service. They could play out the role of the church officer, the flower convener, the church treasurer and the elders.

(vi) A poster might be made as in previous weeks.

(vii) Worksheets are available as an additional activity.

FOURTH WEEK

"THE PEOPLE OF THE CHURCH ARE HELPERS"

Note for teachers

If the programme for the third week was successful it might be repeated this week with different people visiting the various groups. The following stories are available as an alternative programme.

Introduction

YOUNGER SECTION

Remind the children of the people who came to visit the Primary last week. Point out that there are many different ways in which the people of the church can help. Our stories today tell us how some other people are helpers.

FIRST STORY

The telephone rang in Mr. Buchan's house.
"Hello," said Mr. Buchan.
"Hello," said Tom. "Will you help us? We want some men to help to paint the church hall on Saturday afternoon. Will you come and bring your ladder and a paint brush?"
"Yes, I'll be there," said Mr. Buchan. "I'll be glad to help."
On Saturday afternoon he took his ladder and his paint brush to the church hall. He helped Tom and some other people to paint the church hall.
"Now the hall looks bright and clean, ready for the Primary Sunday school," said Mr. Buchan.

Jean was going to the park. On the way she met Miss Lindsay, her Sunday school teacher.

"Hello," said Miss Lindsay.

"Hello," said Jean.

"I'm going to the church to arrange the flowers ready for the service tomorrow," said Miss Lindsay. "Would you like to come and help me?"

"Yes," said Jean, "I should like to help."

At the church, Jean helped to carry the water in a big jug and she helped Miss Lindsay to arrange the flowers in the vases on the Communion table.

"The flowers make the church look beautiful for the service tomorrow," said Jean.

★   ★   ★

Mrs. Andrews was busy shopping in the supermarket when she met Mrs. Hay.

"Good morning," said Mrs. Andrews.

"Good morning," replied Mrs. Hay.

"The minister of our church has just told me that Mrs. Campbell has fallen and broken her arm," said Mrs. Andrews. "I'm looking for people to help her."

"I'll be glad to help," said Mrs. Hay. "I'll call and see what I can do for her."

Every morning Mrs. Hay went shopping and made the beds for Mrs. Campbell until her arm was better again.

★   ★   ★

Jimmy and Bobby were playing at football.

"My Dad's taking me fishing on Saturday," said Jimmy. "Can you come with us?"

"I should like to come," said Bobby, "but I have promised to help to do the garden for old Mrs. Bain. She's far too old to do it herself now and some of the Bible class at the church are going to dig it for her."

"Why don't you let the others do it?" suggested Jimmy. "Then you can come with us. They won't miss you."

"No," said Bobby. "I promised Mrs. Bain I would help to do it this Saturday. She's depending on us."

On Saturday Bobby helped to dig the garden for Mrs. Bain.

Another week he went fishing with Jimmy and his Daddy. They had great fun.

★   ★   ★

Let the children suggest other ways in which the people of the church can help others. The teacher might tell of any project in which their church is engaged.

Lead on to discuss ways in which the children can help. (Perhaps a practical project for helping at home or helping Granny could be discussed and carried out.)

Tell the children that we can all be helpers in the church. Point out that the people of the church are helpers not only in the church building on Sundays but as they help and care for others during the week.

c*

ACTIVITIES

Project 1: The children could help to make something for their own department or a gift for the Nursery group. The following suggestions are given as a guide for the teachers but suggestions from the children should also be incorporated.

(*a*) Markers for the Bible. Pieces of brightly coloured ribbon could be decorated as the table cloth was. (See week 1, p. 66.)

(*b*) A waste paper basket. A cardboard carton or tin might be decorated with scraps from old birthday cards, coloured paper or "fablon."

(*c*) A set of percussion instruments. Tins or polythene detergent bottles of various shapes and sizes, filled with small quantities of peas or rice will make maraccas. (See *The Church Nursery Group,* p. 23.)

Paper cups or ice cream cartons covered with papier mache can also be used.

The children can decorate the instruments with bright colours either with paints or felt pens.

Project 2: The children could make a gift for their Granny or for an old lady in the congregation.

(*a*) A bowl of bulbs could be planted to be distributed when they are flowering.

(*b*) A shopping list. Cut ten or twelve pieces of paper 3″ x 6″, make a cover with thin coloured cardboard, either staple together or tie with ribbon. The children might decorate the cover.

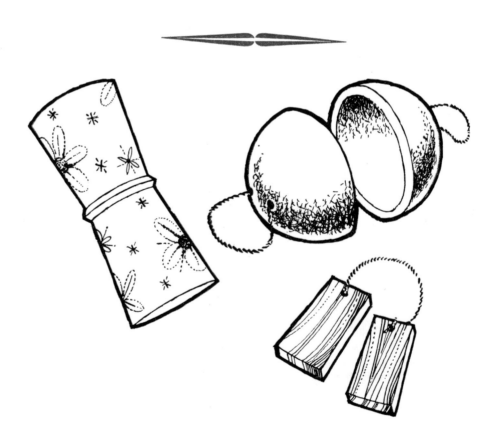

4 Christmas

PREPARING FOR THIS THEME

This theme is concerned with Christmas and therefore it is intended for use during the month of December. Events in the local church at this time may alter the usual pattern of work in the Sunday school but since material for five weeks is given, leaders can select from this.

The Christmas service is the climax of the theme and it is important that it is included.

TIME OF YEAR

The theme aims at helping the children to see that the reason for all the excitement and gladness of Christmas is the coming of Jesus. The starting point of the theme is the children's own experience as they prepare to celebrate Christmas at home and in the church. Teachers must be prepared for the children to be excited about the presents they hope to receive but should try, by providing an opportunity for the making and giving of a gift, to help them to see Christmas not only as a time for receiving presents but also as a time for giving and sharing.

By introducing stories and carols from other countries the children are helped to understand that Christmas is celebrated not only by us, but by Christians in every land. God's revelation of himself in Jesus is not limited to any one class or race, but is for everyone. Christ came to all the world. The story of Siromani reminds us of the challenge to pass on the good news of Christ's coming.

APPROACH TO THEME

Read Is. 9: 2-7. The prophet expresses his firm conviction that deliverance will come to his people. There is evil in the nation and things must be changed; a new nation will evolve through which the will of God will be done. The new kingdom which shall know no end will be ruled over by one who will far excel all previous leaders in wisdom, power and prosperity. This famous passage has been regarded by many as a definite prediction of the coming of Jesus and it has been fulfilled in many ways by him. But the fulfilment of Jesus far exceeds the prophet's expectation and the titles Isaiah uses have taken on for us meanings associated with Jesus rather than Isaiah's original concept.

BIBLICAL FOUNDATIONS
The Prophecy

Now *read John 1: 1-18.* God's love must be expressed. What he does shows his purpose and speaks of his love. This Word brings all things into existence, establishes order and gives life to mankind. John sees Jesus as the clear expression of God's loving purpose coming into the world in answer to man's need. The Word is made flesh. All that Jesus says and all that he does bring light into the darkness of our lives, our ignorance, sin and death. There is no other light and he alone calls us to the new quality of life which God wants us to have.

The true light is there for all men though some do not recognise him. Differences of nationality, race or class, are of no significance. He comes to

The true light

75

banish the darkness for us all. When we "see the light," we recognise that God's love is for us and for everyone; and we respond to that love which affects all our relationships.

A light for all men   The vital connection between the Old Testament and the New is brought out in the story of Simeon and Anna (*see Luke 2: 22-32*). They represent the best of the Old Testament tradition "righteous and devout, looking for the consolation of Israel." But the mission of Jesus is spoken of not in terms of the Jews only; he is to be a light to the Gentiles and so the Saviour of all men.

In this theme we are trying to show that Jesus is given not only to people like us—of our race or way of thinking and customs—but to all varieties of people. His coming creates a new people of God whose thinking and customs are being changed in a revolutionary way as the light of Christ's love is both absorbed and reflected.

PRIMARY WORSHIP

Suitable hymns for this theme will be those used in the Christmas service. It is essential that the children learn "Still the Night" (R.C.H. 49: 1) before the closing worship on the first Sunday of the theme. Other carols from different countries, such as, "Little Jesus, sweetly sleep" (I.P. 62) (Czech) and "Infant Holy, Infant Lowly" (Polish) (page 162) should be introduced. A guitar might be used to accompany some of the carols during this theme. (A Bible class member might be invited to help in this way.)

The Bible reading for the first week might be introduced in the following way. "Today we have been talking about the things we are doing to get ready for Christmas and you have started to make a present to give to your *Mummy*. This is how we celebrate the birth of Jesus. Let's listen again to what it says in the Bible about Jesus' birth." Read Luke 2: 1, 3-7.

Other Bible readings might be: 2nd week—Matt. 2: 9-11; 3rd week—Luke 2: 15-16; 4th week—service; 5th week—Luke 2: 10-11.

THE THEME IN OUTLINE

First week: "Getting ready for Christmas."

The informal talk encourages the children to talk about the things they are doing at home and in the church in preparation for Christmas and provides an introduction to part of the Christmas story read from the R.S.V.

Second week: "Christmas in other lands."

The theme broadens to include Christmas stories and carols from other countries. The younger children have the story of the Austrian carol, "Still the Night" while the older children have the story of Babouschka, a Russian Christmas legend.

Third week: "The Christmas story."

This week is used as a preparation for the Christmas as Service. The Christmas story is read from the R.S.V. after which the children prepare the dramatisation, paintings, models and carols, ready for the Christmas service.

Fourth week: "The Christmas service."

The Christmas service gives the children an opportunity to share actively in worship through drama and music and should be a real and vital experience for them.

Fifth week: "Christmas comes to a village in India."

The story of Siromani shows how a young Indian Christian finds a way of sharing her own Christmas joy with those who have never heard the good news.

NOTE: Where it is felt desirable, "Christmas in other lands" (week two) may be omitted, and two weeks spent on "The Christmas story" (week three) preparing for the service.

Suggestions for the Book Corner

Little Benjamin and the First Christmas, The Secret of the Star, Mary's Story, The Baby Born in a Stable (Arch Books).
Christmas Round the World, Elsie Jones (Lutterworth Press).

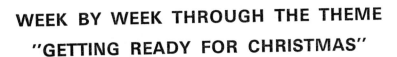

WEEK BY WEEK THROUGH THE THEME
"GETTING READY FOR CHRISTMAS"

FIRST WEEK

Ask the children what is special about this time of year.

BOTH SECTIONS
Informal Talk

Encourage them to talk about the preparations that are being made at home, ready for Christmas. (*Shopping, buying presents, sending cards, putting up decorations, Christmas trees, lights.*)

The children will naturally want to talk about the presents they hope to receive but try to encourage them also to talk about the presents they are planning to give. Point out that Christmas is a time for giving as well as for receiving presents. Ask them if they know why we do all these things at Christmas time.

Point out that this is how we celebrate the *birth* of Jesus. Remind the children that it is because we celebrate the birth of Jesus in the Church that we do all these things.

Ask the children if they know what we do in the church at Christmas.
We sing carols; we have parties; we hear the story of Jesus' birth. (If your church has a special carol service, talk about this.)

Suggest that they listen to what the Bible says about Jesus' birth. *Read Luke 2: 1, 3 and 7* (R.S.V.).

Discuss with the children the present they can make in the Sunday school today and to whom they should give it.

All the activities this week should be concerned with making presents. Teachers should make samples of the presents suggested for the children to see so that they can choose more easily which one they wish to make. Let the children make as much of the present as possible but a little help and guidance from the teacher may be necessary.

ACTIVITIES

(i) *A calendar.* The picture can either be drawn by children with crayons or felt pens or they can be cut out from old Christmas cards or magazines. Glue the picture on to the centre of a paper plate or a cheese box lid. Use Christmas ribbon to make the loop for hanging and for attaching the date tag.

(ii) *A Christmas card.* The children might print their design, using a potato print (see p. 40, *Things to Make* (Ladybird)) or they could use the picture from an old Christmas card, making a design for the border with crayons or felt pens. They could write or glue on a simple greeting inside the card.

(iii) *A Christmas decoration.* Use a plastic jelly case, a small log of wood or a tin lid, for the base. Mix some polyfilla for the centre and before it dries let the children fix a candle, fir cone, twigs, a coloured ball, or tinsel, and a holly leaf into the mixture. (If glue is spread on to the cones and twigs, glitter will stick to it and give a frost effect.)

(iv) *A Christmas mobile.* Fix a piece of coloured cardboard ($1\frac{1}{2}$″ x 24″) into a circle with a brass paper fastener or staple and attach three pieces of string or tinsel to it for hanging up the mobile.

With pieces of fine string of varying lengths, the children can hang some Christmas shapes they have made from this circle.

The swans in the illustration are made from a pipe-cleaner and some angel hair, with a small piece of red plastic tubing for the beak.

The stars and balls were made from coloured foil paper.

(v) *A group project* might be making a Christmas parcel for a family in need. Decorate a fruit basket or large shoe box with crepe paper. Arrange for the children to bring gifts of groceries, fruit and toys to put into the basket. Cover with cellophane paper and attach a Christmas greeting label.

(The local Child Care Officer might be able to supply names of families in special need and deliver the parcels on behalf of the Sunday school.)

(vi) Worksheets provide an extra activity.

"CHRISTMAS IN OTHER LANDS"

Ask the children if they know what we call the special hymns and songs we sing at Christmas time. (*Carols.*)

Ask them which carols they know and if they have a favourite one.

Point out that last Sunday they were learning the carol "Still the Night." Tell them that the story today tells us how that carol was written. (*If the children are familiar with the story suggest that they tell it to you.*)

"THE STORY OF AN AUSTRIAN CAROL"

A long time ago, in a little village in the country of Austria, the boys and girls and grown-up people, too, were getting ready for Christmas.

In the little church on the hill, they had made a model of the Nativity with Mary, Joseph and the baby Jesus, ready for the carol service on Christmas Eve. Now they were busy learning carols and making presents to take to that service.

One evening just before Christmas Eve, Joseph Mohr, the minister, was walking home from the little church. It was getting quite dark. The stars were twinkling in the sky and the fields were covered with fresh white snow.

"How beautiful it is and how still!" thought Joseph Mohr. "It must have been as still and as silent as this when Jesus was born in Bethlehem."

When he reached home, he had his supper. Afterwards, as he sat alone in his study preparing the service for Christmas Eve, he read again the story of the birth of Jesus. "Unto you is born this day in the city of David, a Saviour, which is Christ the Lord."

He could almost see it, the manger in the stable, Joseph and Mary with baby Jesus.

Suddenly he found he was making a poem. "Still the night, holy the night!"

"A carol, a carol," he shouted. "I'm making a *new* carol. It shall be my Christmas present for the children and we will say it together at the Christmas Eve service."

The next morning he took the carol to show to his friend Franz Grüber, the music teacher in the village school.

"I've written a new carol," he told him. "It's my present for the children."

Franz Grüber was as delighted as Joseph Mohr when he read the words of the carol.

"Joseph," he said, "I have thought of a new tune already for your poem. Listen." Joseph listened to the tune and soon he was singing it, too.

"Now the children can sing it in the church on Christmas Eve and it will make your present even better than it was before," said Franz.

Later that day Joseph and Franz arranged a carol practice in the church for all the children in the village.

"I have a new carol for you to sing," said Joseph Mohr. "I wrote it as my Christmas present and Franz Grüber has written a tune for it. We will learn it and sing it as a surprise for all the people in the village. Will you keep the secret?"

"Yes, you know we will," promised the children.

They learned the words quickly but when Franz Grüber tried to play the tune on the organ it would not play.

The organ pipes had got too cold and not a single note would play. What could they do !

"I'll go home for my guitar," said Franz, and he hurried home.

When he returned the children worked hard learning their new carol and their voices rang sweetly through that little church on the hill.

On Christmas Eve, the bells rang calling the people to the service. Joseph Mohr could see lights like twinkling stars, everywhere, as the people carried their lanterns up the hillside to the church, bringing their gifts.

The children had kept the secret and the new carol was a wonderful surprise for their mothers and fathers. They could almost see the stable and Joseph and Mary with the baby Jesus, as the children sang :

"Still the night, holy the night !
Sleeps the world ; hid from sight,
Mary and Joseph in stable bare
Watch o'er the Child beloved and fair,
Sleeping in heavenly rest."

Before long, Joseph Mohr's Christmas present for the children in that Austrian village became a present for people all over the world as they remember the birth of Jesus.

OLDER SECTION
Introduction

Remind the children of the things we do at home and in the church when we remember the birth of Jesus. Point out that in other countries people celebrate his birth in different ways. Our story comes from Russia and it is one that Russian children like to hear every Christmas.

"A RUSSIAN CHRISTMAS LEGEND"

STORY

Long ago, in a little hut on the edge of a great forest lived an old woman. She was called old Babouschka.

One cold winter's night, when the ground was covered with thick snow and the trees in the forest were sparkling with snowflakes, old Babouschka made a big fire in her hut to keep warm. "How glad I am to sit by this warm fire on a cold winter's night," she said.

Suddenly, she heard someone coming. "Who can be coming to visit me on a cold night like this ?" she wondered. There came a knock at the door. Who could it be ?

She got up from her chair and opened the door. There, standing at the door were three strange-looking men, each of them wearing a crown on his head. Babouschka had never seen people dressed as they were dressed.

"They must be kings," she thought.

In their hands they were carrying presents, gold, frankincense and myrrh.

"We are three wise men from a far country," they said. "And we are going to visit a new-born king. Will you come with us to Bethlehem ?"

But old Babouschka shook her head. "No! No!" she said. "The night is cold and the snow is deep and you have rich presents for the king. I am old and poor and have no presents to give him, I cannot go with you to Bethlehem." And so the wise men went on their journey.

After the visitors had gone away Babouschka was sad. She wished she had gone with them.

"But what presents have I for a king?" she said. "The three wise men had gold, frankincense and myrrh, I have none of these. No, I could not go with them."

Then old Babouschka thought again. "They said he was a new-born king. I am sure I could find a present for a baby. Tomorrow I *will* go to Bethlehem."

Early next morning she filled her basket with all the things that she thought a baby would like, coloured balls, strings of shining beads and little animals and dolls carved from wood. She put on her cloak and warm fur boots and set off on her journey.

But which way was it to Bethlehem? Outside her door in the deep, white snow there was not a footprint to be seen to show the way the wise men had gone.

Down into the town she went carrying her basket of toys. "Have you seen three wise men with presents for a new-born king?" she asked all the people she met. But they only smiled and shook their heads.

Babouschka looked everywhere but she could not find the way to Bethlehem.

As she walked home slowly and sadly to her little hut on the edge of the great forest, she saw some children who had no toys.

"I will give the presents that I have for the baby king to these children," she thought. And so she did.

Then every year at Christmas time she went out across the snow with her basket of toys, hoping to find the wise men so that she could take her presents to the new-born king.

Although she looked everywhere she never found her way to Bethlehem but as she journeyed home she always left the toys from her basket for the children.

Since then, on Christmas Eve, Russian boys and girls put their shoes beside the fireplace hoping that Babouschka will fill them with toys. As they open their presents on Christmas morning and remember how Jesus was born in Bethlehem, they say, "Old Babouschka has been and she has brought us the presents that she had for the new-born king."

Our Bible tells us about the wise men who brought presents to Jesus; this is what it says: read Matt. 2: 1-5a and 7-11.

ACTIVITIES

Let the children choose from the following:
(i) Painting. Individual paintings or a group frieze could be made, either of the stories told today or of the Christmas story.

(ii) A collage frieze of the Christmas story would be most effective. Provide cotton wool or scraps of sheep's wool for the sheep, twigs can be fixed on with sellotape to make the shepherd's fire. Brightly coloured foil paper can be used for the wise men.

(iii) A model of the Nativity scene. Use a large cardboard carton for the stable.

To make the figures. Use a polythene bottle for the body and a small paper bag filled with crumpled newspaper or an old ball for the head. Fix the head to the body with a strong glue or brown gummed paper. Pieces of scrap material can be fixed to the figures for clothes and crowns made from foil paper.

Draw on the features with felt pens and use sheep's wool or rug wool for the hair. The animals can be made from plasticine, dough or clay.

(iv) Lanterns. Some children might make lanterns to use during the Christmas service. (See p. 85.) Cover a cardboard carton with white paper, draw or use coloured paper for the windows (see diagram), and fix the top of the carton to a piece of dowel or cane.

(v) Dramatisation. The stories which have been told today can be dramatised or the children might prefer to dramatise the Christmas story.

(vi) An additional activity for the older children might be the making of a scrapbook or frieze of "Christmas in other lands." The book, *Christmas Round the World*, by Elsie Jones, can be used for the children's own research. Stories, prayers and carols might be included in this book.

(vii) An Advent wreath. Some of the older children might be interested in preparing an Advent wreath for the worship centre. (See page 2, *Christmas Round the World*.) Four candles, strong wire, some evergreen and ribbon are required for this.

(viii) The worksheets can be used by both sections for individual work.

"THE CHRISTMAS STORY"

The Christmas service is the climax of this theme and this week might be used in preparing for that service. It is assumed that the service will be carried out in the hall where the Primary usually meets and that the children will share actively in the worship through the dramatisation and singing.

The following procedure is suggested:
The Primary should be divided into six main groups for the Christmas service. The groups can either be the usual class groups or groups specially arranged for the occasion. Three groups, consisting of the younger children should be responsible for the first three scenes. The three other groups from the older section should cope more easily with scene 4, the readings and the choir.
(In a small Primary, scene 4 and choir could be omitted and the older children included in the other scenes.)
All the children should be involved in the service in some way. The value lies in the participation by the children, not in a polished performance.
The teachers should know in advance which group they are responsible for so that they can make their preparations for such things as dressing-up materials and stage props.

Scenes 1, 2 and 3 might be prepared as follows:
(1) In the group, the teacher should recall the story or scene to be dramatised. (Using the R.S.V.) Discuss the people in the story. The children can choose the part they want to play. They are usually good at deciding who will make a good innkeeper or wise man.

(2) The children should be encouraged to make their own suggestions for the dramatisation, which should be imaginative and unscripted. The teacher should guide their suggestions but must avoid over-directing the action. She should also resist the temptation to put words into the children's mouths but speech which arises spontaneously as the children act should be encouraged.
Some children may prefer to mime rather than speak the part.

(3) Dressing-up materials and a few stage "props" will enrich the dramatisation. If materials such as old curtains, scarves, towels, squares of material for head-dresses are provided, the children can help each other to choose how their character is to be dressed. (Head-dresses can be held in place by the stretch welt of nylon stockings or pieces of wide ribbon or braid.) Simple props can be made by the children if the right materials are provided by the teacher. The wise men could make their crowns and gifts, other children could make the shepherd's fire and the manger.

(4) The scene should be rehearsed in preparation for the Christmas service.

Scene 4. Some of the older children who wrote stories about Christmas in other lands last Sunday might prepare parts of this to be included in the Christmas service. They should write out the story in their own words and practise saying it aloud. They might also prepare some dramatisation for this scene.

Readers. These children should copy out the words they have to speak on a piece of paper. (The leader should have a duplicate copy in case the children forget to bring their copy next Sunday.) The children need not learn the words but the service will be more effective if they read the words well. The readings are taken from the R.S.V. and it would be helpful if the children read directly from this version of the Bible for the service.

Choir. The service includes a number of carols. Those who choose to be in the choir should practise the hymns and carols to be sung. They might also copy out the words of some of the carols and make their own book of carols.

FOURTH WEEK   ## "THE CHRISTMAS SERVICE"

Allow time for each group to dress up and practice the scene before meeting together. When the groups are ready, gather the children together in their groups, either in a large semi-circle or on three sides of a square. Leave plenty of space at the front and in the middle of the room for the dramatisation.

SERVICE

Leader:	O come let us adore Him,
	O come let us adore Him, Christ the Lord.
	At Christmas time the people of the Church in many lands remember the birth of Jesus. In our service we are going to sing some of the carols which came to us from other lands.
All sing:	"Still the Night" (R.C.H. 49 : 1) Austrian carol.
Leader:	Prayer. (One that the children have written during this theme might be used.)

Scene 1—   Going to Bethlehem.

1st reader:	Luke 2 : 1-3 (R.S.V.).
All sing:	"Here we go up to Bethlehem" (p. 160).
Dramatisation:	The people going to Bethlehem can skip and dance as they sing this carol.
2nd reader:	Luke 2 : 4-5a.
Dramatisation:	Mary and Joseph make their way to Bethlehem. Joseph knocks on doors asking the innkeepers for a room. The last one finds room for them in the stable.
A carol:	Read by a group of children :
	"No room, no room in the inn tonight
	For Mary and Joseph and Holy Light;
	No room in the inn for a Baby's birth,
	No room for the King of heaven and earth." [1]
All sing:	"Still the Night" (R.C.H. 49 : 1).
3rd reader:	Luke 2 : 6-7.
All sing:	"Little Jesus, sweetly sleep" (I.P. 62) Czech carol.

[1] From *A Carol Service for Children* by Herbert Greig, Chappell & Co. Ltd.

Scene 2— **The shepherds hear the Good News.**
4th reader: Luke 2: 8-9.
Dramatisation: Shepherds sitting around the fire, guarding the sheep.
5th reader: Luke 2: 10-12.
Dramatisation: Shepherds afraid and cover their faces. Then listen to the good news of Jesus' birth.
6th reader: Luke 2: 13.
A group of children say or sing "Glory to God in the highest, and on earth, peace, goodwill toward men."
7th reader: Luke 2: 15-16.
Dramatisation: The shepherds hurry to Bethlehem.
All sing: "Infant Holy, Infant lowly," Polish carol (p. 162).

Scene 3— **The wise men bring their gifts.**
8th reader: Matt. 2: 9b, 10-11.
All sing: "The wise men came from out of the East" (p. 161).
Dramatisation: The wise men follow the star to Bethlehem and present their gifts.

Scene 4— **People in many lands celebrate Christmas.**
All sing: "Still the Night" (R.C.H. 49: 1).
(The children who made lanterns could have a procession around the room.)
Leader: "Colin" and "Janet" are going to tell us in their own words how Christmas is celebrated in other lands, and then "Mrs. Adair's" class will act out the story.
All sing: "Baby Jesus, sleeping softly" (I.P. 60) or repeat one of the other carols.
Leader: Prayer:
"We thank you, God, for all the fun we have at Christmas time. Help us to share our happiness with other people." Amen.
All sing: "Away in a Manger" (R.C.H. 657).

"CHRISTMAS COMES TO A VILLAGE IN INDIA"

FIFTH WEEK

BOTH SECTIONS

Introduction

Allow the children time to talk about the presents they have received this Christmas. Tell the children that even though people in many countries remember Jesus' birth at Christmas time, there are still boys and girls and grown-ups, too, who have never heard of Jesus. Our story tells us how Christmas came to the people in a village in India.

STORY

It was Christmas Eve in a village in India but not one of the boys and girls seemed to know it. There wasn't a Christmas tree or any decorations to be seen anywhere. The boys and girls played out in the streets just as they did on any other day. No-one in that village had ever heard the story of Jesus being born in Bethlehem, no-one knew about the shepherds who came to visit him and the wise men who brought him their presents.

But although the children in that village in India knew nothing about it when they went to bed on Christmas Eve, Christmas *had* come to the village. There had been a wedding in one of the little houses at the very end of the village street. The young man who lived there had just married a very beautiful young girl from a town some miles away. Her name was Siromani. She had made friends with the boys and girls in the village and knew each one of them and where they lived.

On this Christmas Eve Siromani was feeling very sad. She was wishing she could spend Christmas with her friends in the town.

"It won't be like Christmas at all," she thought. "Nobody in this village even knows about Christmas. There won't be any carols or presents or anything."

Then suddenly she had an idea. "If nobody knows about Christmas, I could tell them. If these boys and girls have never had a happy Christmas then they shall have one tomorrow."

And she hurried off to the little shop in the village and bought some butter, sugar and some coconut.

On returning to her house she lit the fire and put on the biggest cooking pot she could find. Soon there was a lovely smell of cooking. In between the cooking and the stirring, Siromani made some pretty little paper bags from some brightly coloured paper. When the sugary, nutty sweets were cooked and cooled, she put some into each bag and tied them up with gold tinsel.

She counted her bags carefully saying, "There are two boys in that home and a girl in the next, and in that one there are two girls and a baby." And so she went on until she had made a present of sweets for every boy and girl in the village. It took her a long time, but when she had made enough she piled the bags on to her big brass tray and set off round the village.

By this time all the boys and girls were fast asleep in their beds. When she came to the first house the door was shut. She knocked softly.

"Who is there?" called someone from inside.

"Christmas is here!" laughed Siromani.

The mother of the home opened the door and peeped out. Siromani gave her the gay parcels and said, "Here are three Christmas presents. Give them to the children in the morning. Happy Christmas!"

Off she went to the next house. Knock! knock! "Happy Christmas! Give these to the children in the morning."

Then to the next home. Knock! knock! "Happy Christmas! This is the day when we remember the birth of Jesus in Bethlehem," she told the mother.

When all the bags of sweets had been delivered, Siromani knew that every boy and girl in the village had a surprise waiting for them on Christmas morning.

"It will be a lovely Christmas after all," she said as she went to bed.

On Christmas morning all the children came to thank Siromani for the sweets she had made for them. "But what is Christmas?" they asked. "Tell us about Christmas."

So on that Christmas morning those Indian boys and girls sat listening for the first time to the story of how Jesus was born, long ago in Bethlehem and how he is the friend of all.

The next Christmas it wasn't just Siromani who shared her Christmas presents, all the boys and girls made presents for each other and for their mummies and daddies, just as we do.

Painting and dramatisation could be attempted this week but allow time for the children to sing the carols they have been learning throughout this theme.

The worksheets should be completed and taken home.

ACTIVITIES

(The story of Siromani is freely adapted from the story "How Christmas came to a village in India," in *The Pilgrim Elementary Teacher*. The Pilgrim Press. Used by permission.)

5 God's world in winter

PREPARING FOR THIS THEME

TIME OF YEAR This theme is intended for use in January when Scotland is usually still in the grips of winter.

APPROACH TO THEME The theme begins by looking with the children at the world around them in winter in town or country and exploring with them some of the sights, sounds and things they enjoy doing in winter.

As the theme develops it leads the children to say "thank you" to God for those who look after them in winter and for all the things they enjoy.

But winter is sometimes a difficult time for birds and people and therefore stories about caring for birds and people in winter are introduced to show man's part in caring for God's world. As we think of those who care for us we are reminded of our responsibility towards those in need.

Finally, on the fourth Sunday, the things the children have made, written and painted and their dramatisation about the world in winter are offered to God in an act of worship.

BIBLICAL FOUNDATIONS
It is God's world The Psalms are rich in material for this theme and they show us how man saw God in the world in which he lived and was alive to the beauty and order of nature. *Read Ps. 65: 5-13*. In this passage the psalmist sees the whole earth praising God in all places and at all times. God is not remote from this world but is its controller and sustainer.

Winter is part of the natural order in the world which is God's creation. Ps. 74: 17—"Thou hast fixed all the bounds of the earth: thou hast made summer and winter." Gen. 8: 22—"While the earth remains, seedtime and harvest, cold and heat, summer and winter, day and night shall not cease."

But winter brings its problems for animals and birds and we should try to help them. Gen. 1 : 28b—"Have dominion over the fish of the sea and over the birds of the air and over every living thing."

This is an indication of our responsibility.

Concern for the needs of others Winter can be hard for people too. The Bible makes God's concern for the well-being of his people quite clear, and repeatedly they are reminded that they should care for others. There is no real appreciation of God's love for us, nor any proper response to it, if we do not care about others.

"If anyone has the world's goods and sees his brother in need, yet closes his heart against him, how does God's love abide in him?" (I John 3 : 17.)

"If God so loved us, we also ought to love one another." (1 John 4 : 11.)

Who is my neighbour? *Read Luke 10: 25-27*. When Jesus was asked, "Who is my neighbour?" his answer makes it quite clear that he does not concern himself with this kind of limiting question but says, "You are the neighbour, go and be one."

88

PRIMARY WORSHIP

A suitable hymn for the theme is "All creatures of our God and King" (R.C.H. 13 : 1).

Other appropriate hymns are: "All things bright and beautiful" (I.P. 1); "Little birds in winter-time" (Tune: Child Songs 93); "To God who makes all lovely things" (I.P. 13 : 1, 3 and 5); "All the flowers are sleeping" (I.P. 82 : 4).

Bible readings. On the third Sunday of this theme the leader might introduce the Bible reading in the following way. "On our tape recorder we have just heard some of the children saying 'thank you' to God for those who look after them in winter. In the Bible it says, 'If God so loved us, we also ought to love one another.' (1 John 4 : 11.) We are going to show our love to others by giving the offerings we have brought today to the Church of Scotland Children's Homes."

Other Bible readings might include: Ps. 147 : 16; Job 37 : 6a; Gen. 8 : 22.

THE THEME IN OUTLINE

First week: Looking at the world in winter.

The stories of the little frog for the younger section and of Kofi from Africa for the older section are used to encourage the children to talk about their own experiences of winter.

Second week: Feeding the birds.

A modern story of feeding the birds in winter in which the younger children can identify themselves with the children in the story encourages them to look after the birds in winter. For the older children the story of St. Francis and how he cared for all living things, particularly the birds, reminds us that we should look after the birds and animals in winter-time.

Third week: Caring for others in winter a long time ago.

Some people do not have a warm home, with a cosy fire to keep them warm in winter. Long ago many orphans and others had to roam the streets looking for a place to stay the night. The story of Dr. Barnardo for the younger section and St. Margaret for the older section tell how they cared for such children.

Fourth week: A "thank you" service.

This week all the material that has been prepared over the last three weeks is used in an act of worship about "God's world in winter."

Suggestions for the Book Corner

What to look for in winter, Garden birds (Ladybird).

Praise Him (Mowbrays).

The Robin, The Blackbird (W. & R. Chambers Ltd.).

Hot and Cold, Fur and Feather (A. & C. Black, London).

Pictures of winter scenes, robins and other birds and people dressed in warm winter clothes could be made into a scrapbook for the Book Corner.

**NOTE TO
TEACHERS**

A leaflet giving details for making a bird table will be sent free to children or teachers who send a stamped addressed envelope to—Royal Society for the Protection of Birds, The Lodge, Sandy, Bedfordshire. The instructions are easy to follow and the materials needed are inexpensive. The leaflet also gives advice on how to feed birds.

Information about people who care for others can be obtained from— The Committee on Social Service, 121 George Street, Edinburgh EH2 4YN; Dr. Barnardo's, 22 Drumsheugh Gardens, Edinburgh, EH3 7RP; National Children's Home, Highbury Park, London, N.5; Quarrier's Homes, Bridge of Weir.

FIRST WEEK

WEEK BY WEEK THROUGH THE THEME
LOOKING AT THE WORLD IN WINTER

**YOUNGER
SECTION
STORY**

Once upon a time there was a little frog who wanted to see winter. Usually in the autumn he went down to the bottom of the big pond and there he slept until it was spring again. One chilly autumn day, as he sat on the edge of the pond, all the other frogs swam to the bottom to sleep.

"Goodbye," he called to them, "I'm going to stay here to see what winter is like."

After all the other frogs had gone the little frog began to feel sleepy.

"I'll just go down to the bottom of the pond for a quick sleep," he said, "then I'll come back to the top of the pond tomorrow and wait to see winter." But when the little frog came back again to the top of the pond he discovered that he had slept for a long time. It was spring again and he still didn't know about winter.

**Children
participate**

Ask the children to tell you what the little frog would have seen if he stayed at the top of the pond and seen winter. (*Bare branches, a few leaves on the ground, frost, ice, snow.*)

Ask them what games the children would be playing (*snowballs, sliding, making snowmen*) and what kind of clothes the people would be wearing (*boots, gloves, scarves, warm woollen and fur clothing*).

**OLDER SECTION
STORY**

Kofi and his family lived in Africa. One day a letter arrived for Kofi's father telling him that he had been offered a new job in Scotland and all the family could go to live there.

When they arrived at the airport in Scotland it was winter. In Africa it was usually very hot and Kofi and his family had never seen winter before.

**Children
participate**

How would they know it was winter and not summer? (*Snow, ice, cold, bare trees.*)

What kind of clothes do you think they would need to buy? (*Gloves, warm clothes made of fur or woollen material, fur boots, scarves, tights.*)

Ask the children what they themselves enjoy most about winter.

If possible arrange for groups of children to go out of doors to look at the world in winter.

In school the children may have been hearing about hibernation. Encourage them to tell what they know about animals and birds in winter.

Suggest that during the next week the children put out food for the birds and on the following Sunday talk about the birds they have seen.

Before the children begin their activities read to them from the Bible what someone a long time ago had to say about winter (Ps. 147 : 16, "God gives snow like wool ; he scatters hoarfrost like ashes.")

(i) A collage frieze of a winter scene. A group of children could draw or paint the background and then by using cotton wool to represent snow ; glitter or milk bottle tops for frost ; matchboxes glued on to the background for houses with cotton wool or white towelling material to represent snow-covered roofs, this could be a three-dimensional frieze. The figures could be dressed in woollen or fur material.

(ii) A model of a winter scene. A baking tin or tray can be used for the base with a foundation of white towelling material or strong paper. Trees can be made from bare twigs set in plasticine ; houses from cartons of various sizes ; foil paper or a mirror for the frozen lake ; and pipe-cleaner figures can be made and dressed in warm winter clothes.

(iii) Individual pictures can be made by children who like to work alone. These can be included in a scrapbook on "The World in Winter."

(iv) Writing. "Things I like about winter." These could include Christmas holidays, playing with new toys, playing out in the snow, which could then be grouped by the teacher to form part of the act of worship.

(v) Dramatisation. A group of children might like to mime or make a dance about a cold day in winter. (*Putting on warm clothes, playing out in the snow.*)

(vi) Worksheets. Use can be made of these.

FEEDING THE BIRDS

Ask the children if they have been feeding the birds. Were they hungry ?

What did they like to eat ?

What kind of birds did you see ?

(If possible, show pictures of the birds they see in Scotland during the winter months to help with identification.)

" PETER FEEDS THE BIRDS "

Peter was five years old, and he asked questions all day long. "Why does the dog wag its tail?" "Where does the rain come from?" "Why can't I stay up all night?" He started asking questions almost as soon as he opened his eyes in the morning. But Peter was lucky, he had a big sister Anne who was eight years old and she liked to help to answer Peter's questions.

One cold winter's morning when Peter and Anne were just going to have their breakfast, Peter said, "It's my turn to say grace," and so he sang "Thank you for the world so sweet . . ." Then he asked, "Do all boys and girls say thank you for their porridge?" Anne took a spoonful of porridge and then replied, "We all say 'thank you' to God for our dinner in school. Don't we?"

That satisfied Peter for a few minutes until he heard a bird singing outside the window. "What's that?" he asked.

"That's a robin," Daddy said.

"Can I go and see?" Peter said, but Mummy told him to finish his breakfast first or he'd be late for school.

Anne knew about robins and she said to Peter, "A robin is a little brown bird with a red breast."

"Yes, I know," said Peter. "I've seen him often in our garden."

"We'll go and look for him before we go to school," suggested Anne.

Now Peter was ready with another question before he took a bite of his roll. "Is he saying 'thank you' for his breakfast?"

"Poor robin," said Daddy. "He won't have much to eat this cold weather. All summer he eats insects and slugs in the garden but now the ground is hard and covered with frost. He'll be hungry often."

"He can have some of my breakfast," said Peter.

"When you've finished," said Mummy, "we'll give him some crumbs. He'll like that."

After breakfast, just before it was time for Peter and Anne to leave for school, they put on their boots and warm scarves, fastened up their duffel coats and went out to feed the robin. They scattered some crumbs that they had saved from their rolls and put down a saucer filled with water. From the branch of a tree the robin watched them with his bright little eyes on the crumbs.

"Come inside now," said Anne. "The robin may be afraid to come down while we're here."

Sure enough, when Peter and Anne went inside, down came robin and began to pick up the crumbs.

"Poor robin," said Peter. "He hasn't warm clothes like us to wear in winter."

"But his feathers keep him warm," said Anne.

Soon the robin had finished his breakfast and began to sing again. "There," said Peter as he and Anne hurried off to school, "he's saying 'thank you' for his breakfast. We'll put out some crumbs for him every day."

"FRANCIS CARES FOR ANIMALS AND BIRDS"

OLDER SECTION

Introduction

As for the younger section.

In winter when the ground is hard the birds cannot get enough food to eat. When we feed them we are helping to take care of the birds in winter. Today we are going to hear a story of a man who loved all birds and animals.

STORY

Once upon a time there lived in Italy a rich, young man called Francis. Francis had everything that money could buy—a fine house, beautiful clothes, a strong horse to ride on, and a great many rich friends.

One day when Francis had ridden a long way from home, he felt sure that there was work he must do. He must become a friend to those who had no friends and help people who were sick and poor just as Jesus did. So Francis went home, left his rich friends and gave away all his money to help the poor. He took off his fine clothes and put on a long brown robe, like a dressing gown, that almost touched the ground when he walked. Round his waist he wore a rope like a belt. He helped many people who were sick and became a friend of those who had no friends. There was always plenty of work for Francis to do and he was happier now than he had ever been before.

One day he went to a place called Assisi. There he gathered round him others who wanted to help him in his work. Francis and his friends were called the Brothers and anyone who needed help went to them.

Once, when Francis was walking along a road, he met a boy who was taking a cage of white doves to sell in the market. The doves were frightened because the cage was so small they could not fly about in it like your budgie does in his.

"Your doves are far too beautiful to be shut up in a cage. Will you give them to me?" asked Francis.

The boy looked at the doves in the cage and then at Francis.

"I am sure you will know how to look after them properly," he said, "so you can have them."

Francis put his hand into the cage and very carefully took out the birds. He spoke to them quietly and then set them free. At first they flew up and up into the air. Then they swooped down to rest on Francis' shoulder and to eat some food from his hand.

No bird or animal was ever afraid of Francis. He used to speak to the birds and tell them to sing and praise God.

Have you heard the birds sing as though they are bursting with happiness? Perhaps they sing a song for you after you have fed them.

Francis wrote a hymn about praising God. It begins:

"All creatures of our God and King,
Lift up your voice and with us sing,
Alleluia."

Suggest that they learn the first verse ready for the closing worship.

ACTIVITIES

(i) A frieze. The children could paint or make a collage picture of Francis surrounded by the animals and birds he loved. An effective way of making a picture so that it resembles a stained glass window is for the children to draw an outline and then fill it in with pieces of coloured paper.

(ii) Wonder table. Some children may like to look at the bulbs to see if they are growing. If possible have at least one bulb growing in water as this allows the children to watch the growth "underground" as well as above ground. Remind the children that the flowers are sleeping in the soil during the winter.

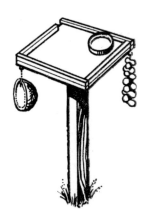

(iii) Feeding the birds. Arrange for some of the children to go out of doors to feed the birds in winter. Crumbs and scraps of fat should be available.

Peanuts could be threaded on to a string for the tits. A handyman in the congregation or a member of the Bible class might help to fix up a bird table in the church grounds.

(iv) The model of the winter scene should be continued.

(v) Dramatisation. The stories of Peter feeding the robin and of Francis can be dramatised.

(vi) Writing. Some children might write a story about feeding the birds in winter or looking after their pets in winter. This could be used in the "thank you" service.

(vii) Worksheets. Use can be made of these.

NOTE

If music is played during the uplifting of the offering, the pianist might play "Feed the Birds" from "Mary Poppins." A recording of this music could be used if there is no pianist. Ask the children to listen quietly whilst it is played.

CARING FOR OTHERS IN WINTER A LONG TIME AGO

"DR. BARNARDO CARES FOR OTHERS"

Last week we heard how Peter and Anne helped to look after the birds in winter. Ask the children if they remembered to feed the birds this week.

Today we are going to hear the story of a young man who helped some boys and girls who had no-one to care for them, no-one to see that they had warm clothes and plenty of food in winter.

A long time ago, in the city of London, there lived a man called Thomas Barnardo. Thomas was learning to be a doctor because he wanted to go to China, a land far across the sea, to help people who were ill and to tell them about Jesus.

Thomas was very busy studying during the day but at night he had a school for children. Night is a strange time to go to school but in those days many boys and girls like you had to go to work during the day. Thomas Barnardo taught those children in a warm room with a big fire. Many children came wearing ragged clothes and they were glad to be able to crowd into this cosy room at night. One cold winter's night when school was over, Thomas was looking round to see that everyone had gone home when he noticed a small boy huddled in a corner by the fire.

"Come along, Jim," he said, "it's time you were off home."

"Please sir," said Jim, "don't send me out in the cold. Let me sleep here for the night."

"But your father and mother will be worried about you at home, won't they?" asked Thomas.

When the boy replied, "I have no mother or father and no home to go to," Thomas could hardly believe his ears. When Jim told him there were other children who had no-one to take care of them, he hurried out into the cold winter's night to find them. But Jim was right and that night Dr. Barnardo found many boys and girls who had no-one to look after them. He gave them some food, warm clothes and a home to live in with someone in charge to look after them.

OLDER SECTION

STORY

"ST. MARGARET CARES FOR OTHERS"

A long time ago, one stormy morning, a fisherman was walking along the shore, watching the high waves. He was wondering if it would be safe to go out in his little boat. Suddenly he saw a ship tossing on the sea. He watched it very carefully until it had passed the jagged rocks and reached the shallow water. He was very surprised to see a beautiful lady come ashore.

"I am Princess Margaret of England," she said.

"You are in Scotland now," said the fisherman. "King Malcolm's land."

"Then take me to your king," said Princess Margaret. "We have had to leave our land and we hoped to find somewhere to live here."

When King Malcolm saw Princess Margaret he thought she was the most beautiful lady he had ever seen, and he asked her to marry him. And so she became Queen Margaret of Scotland.

Soon the people of Scotland came to know her. She lived in Edinburgh and if you have ever been there you will have seen the castle built upon a rock. The castle where King Malcolm and Queen Margaret lived stood in that very place. You can see a little building there that was built for Queen Margaret. It is a tiny church and is called Queen Margaret's Chapel. Queen Margaret used to go there every day to think about God and ask him to help her to love others as Jesus did.

There were many poor people in Edinburgh and Queen Margaret wanted to help them. Every day at 12 o'clock the doors of the castle were opened wide and poor men, women and children were welcomed into the castle. Queen Margaret gave something to everyone—food for the hungry; money for the poor; clothes for the ragged and medicine for the sick.

She liked to comfort anyone who needed her help but she specially loved little children. Many boys and girls who had no mother and father used to live with her in the castle. She looked after them as if they were her very own children. She often told them stories about Jesus and how he loved children, too.

Ask the children at what time of year the boys and girls and men and women would most appreciate Queen Margaret's help. Why?

Queen Margaret lived a long time ago but the followers of Jesus today are still caring for children who need food and warm clothes and someone to look after them.

The children participate

(i) Frieze. The children could paint or make a collage picture of boys and girls sitting round a fire or a picture of children in their warm beds at night. Others could paint a picture of Queen Margaret caring for people.

ACTIVITIES

(ii) Individual drawings or paintings could be made of people who care for us in winter.

(iii) If a tape recorder is available, a recording could be made of some of the children saying "thank you" for the things they enjoy and for those who care for them in winter. This could be used in the act of worship next Sunday.

(iv) Dramatisation. The younger group could dramatise Dr. Barnardo finding the homeless children. The older group might dramatise the story of Queen Margaret.

(v) Writing. Prayers written by the children saying "thank you" for the people who care for them in winter could be incorporated in the scrapbook.

(vi) Worksheets. Use could be made of these.

(vii) A practical project. In Primaries where the children have plenty of warm clothes suggest that they bring some of the warm clothes they have grown out of to make up a parcel to give to one of the local health visitors for a family who need help. An alternative project might be to send the offering this week for the work of the Church of Scotland Children's Homes which are situated in Edinburgh, Glasgow, Stonehaven, Kilmarnock, Rutherglen and Galashiels. (See address on p. 90.)

A "THANK YOU" SERVICE

FOURTH WEEK

The children should spend a short time in groups with their teachers preparing the work for the service. There should be material from the stories of St. Francis, Dr. Barnardo and Queen Margaret. The models, friezes and individual pictures should be displayed and children's writings prepared for display. The dramatisation and readings should also be prepared.

Preparing for the service

D

SERVICE

Hymn:	"All things bright and beautiful" (I.P. 1).
1st Reader	Gen. 8:22—"While the earth remains, seedtime and harvest, cold and heat, summer and winter, day and night, shall not cease."
2nd Reader:	Job 37:6a and Ps. 147:16—"God said to the snow, be on the earth. He gives snow like wool. He scatters hoarfrost like ashes."

Winter

Ask the children to bring forward the models and paintings they have made.

Leader:	"Helen" is going to read a poem that she has written about winter. (This poem was written by a Primary child for the "thank you" service in her Primary.)

> "Winter snow is falling softly,
> Over hills and dales:
> Falling on the roof-tops,
> Falling on the chimney pots.
> The birds they need some crusts and crumbs,
> On a winter's day."

Dramatisation:	A group of children mime or dance about winter.
Prayer:	Use the tape recording of the children saying "thank you" for the things they enjoy in winter.
Hymn:	"On winter nights his quiet flakes" (I.P. 13, verse 3, then verse 1).
Narrator 1:	Francis loved all birds and animals. He spoke to the birds and told them to sing and praise God.
Narrator 2:	One day Francis met a boy carrying a cage of white doves to sell in the market. He asked the boy to give him the birds. When the boy did so, Francis opened the cage and set the birds free.
Dramatisation:	A group of children dramatise the story of St. Francis.
Hymn:	"All creatures of our God and King" (R.C.H. 13:1).
Narrator 3:	When we feed the birds we are helping God to look after the world in winter.

Feeding the birds

Ask the children to bring forward their paintings about feeding the birds and also examples of the kind of food they give to the birds.

Leader:	"Martin" is going to read to us the story he has written about feeding the birds in winter.
Hymn:	"Little birds in winter time." (Tune: *Child Songs* 93.)

Caring for others in winter

Narrator 4: A long time ago, a young man called Thomas Barnardo helped boys and girls who had no-one to look after them. He gave them warm clothes to wear, beds to sleep in and good food to eat. (The story of Queen Margaret might be used instead of or as well as Dr. Barnardo.)

Dramatisation: The story of Dr. Barnardo.

Narrator 5: Since that winter's night, many homes have been built and people still give money so that Dr. Barnardo's homes can care for boys and girls.

Offering

Prayer: (Taken by leader.) Thank you, God, for those who look after us in winter.

Thank you for our cosy beds and warm fires.

Thank you for the clothes we wear to keep us warm.

Help us to remember those who do not have enough food to eat or clothes to keep them warm in winter. Show us how we can help them. Amen.

Hymn: "He made the people that I meet" (I.P. 13:5).

Leader: Now we are going to hear some words from the Bible.

(Ps. 104:10-14, 16-19, 33—adapted for Primary children.)

"God makes springs of water in the valleys; they flow between the hills, they give drink to the animals.

Near them the birds of the air live and sing among the branches. The trees get plenty of water and in them the birds build their nests. The high mountains are for the wild deer, the woods are for the badgers. The moon marks the seasons and the sun knows its time for setting.

"O Lord, how wonderful are the things you have made: the earth is full of your good gifts. I will sing praise to you as long as I live; I will sing praise to you for ever."

Hymn: "To God who makes all lovely things" (I.P. 13:1, 3 and 5).

6 Choosing

PREPARING FOR THIS THEME

TIME OF YEAR   This theme does not reflect any seasonal interest and could be used at any time of the year. In this programme it is suggested for use in February.

APPROACH TO THEME   The Primary child is already making many choices each day. He chooses his friends and the games he plays, whether to agree or disagree, whether to do what other people tell him to do or not. At this stage of his development he is basically egocentric. He is more concerned with himself and what he does and usually chooses the biggest and best for himself. Christian upbringing involves the development of right attitudes towards other people and of a true appreciation of our own contribution to the well-being of society.

Children need the opportunity to exercise freedom of choice if they are to develop a sense of responsibility and establish good relationships. This theme attempts to help the children to understand the rights of others to choose and encourages them to think about some of the choices they make.

In this theme we see the disciples choosing to follow Jesus and by means of a modern missionary story how people choose to follow him today.

BIBLICAL FOUNDATIONS   The main emphasis of both Old and New Testaments is upon God's choice of individuals and of people to serve him in particular situations. His choice is not conditioned by external factors, but it is in real-life situations that he initiates action to achieve his purpose. His nature is revealed and his love is expressed in what he does. People are free to respond to him, to accept or reject his rule over them. *See Deut. 30: 15-20; Matt. 5: 18-24 and 9: 9.*

Choice in the Bible   We find people making choices in many passages, and the rightness and wrongness of their choice is seen in the light of the writer's understanding of the nature of God. Sometimes it is through the consequences of the choice that insight is gained into the purpose of God, and sometimes the choice expresses what is believed to be the will of God. E.g., Abraham and Lot, Gen. 13; Ruth 1: 16-18; Acts 1: 21-26, 15: 36-40.

Our choices   We have to make choices every day. Sometimes our choice is decided by our past, our environment, our experiences, our prejudices or dispositions, but for the Christian there should always be another factor: "Lord, what would you have me do?" and this should appear in what we decide to do with the talents and possessions which God has given to us. Our decision "for Christ" does not make all other decisions automatic or easy. To follow him means to obey him even when it is difficult, to allow him to rule in matters which many regard as their own business, to accept his way completely, not to select those aspects of his nature that we find agreeable to our inclinations. *See Matt. 7: 21-23 and John 15: 14-17.*

Our response to God will be seen as we choose to follow the way of Christ in the opportunities and situations which open to us. Our creed is not seen mainly in what we say, but in what we do—in our respect for others and for the life and gifts we have been given. Luke 14 : 16-21 ; Matt. 25 : 14-36 ; 1 Cor. 12 : 4-11.

We make wrong choices sometimes, of course (even when we choose to do nothing), either by mistake or simply because we are sinners. In Christ there is a remedy (1 John 1 : 8-9). We may be forgiven, grow in our understanding of Christ's way and begin to make better choices.

PRIMARY WORSHIP

The song for the theme might be "Happy Thought" (p. 164). Other hymns for this theme can be chosen from the following—"Saviour, teach me" (R.C.H. 437 : 1-2) ; "In Galilee beside the sea" (I.P. 69) ; "When Jesus saw the fishermen" (S.H.P.C.) ; "Jesus, Friend of little children" (R.C.H. 667) ; "Far round the World" (R.C.H. 373).

The Bible reading for the third week might be introduced in the following way. "In your groups you heard how the disciples chose to help Jesus. Now I'm going to read that story again from the Bible." *Read Matt. 4: 18-22.*

Other Bible readings might include—Gen. 13: 8-9 ; Matt. 9: 9 ; John 15 : 16-17 ; Matt. 25 : 40b.

THE THEME IN OUTLINE

First week: "Choosing the things we like."
The theme begins by giving the children an opportunity to choose and to discuss some of the choices they make each day.

Second week: "Making choices."
In this story Jesus told, we look at the choices that the various characters make.

Third week: "The disciples choose to follow Jesus."
The theme now focuses upon Jesus calling his disciples and the four fishermen and Matthew are taken as examples of those who choose to help him.

Fourth week: "Choosing to follow Jesus today."
The story of Louisa Cowie and her work as a nurse in Southern Yemen shows that people today choose to be followers of Jesus.

Suggestions for the Book Corner
Our Book Corner, 3rd shelf—"Men and Women at Work" series, *The Doctor and the Nurse* (Chambers).
The Nurse; The Fisherman (Ladybird "People at Work" series).
The House on the Rock; Eight Bags of Gold (Arch Books).

Useful reference book:
Life in New Testament Times (Ladybird).

WEEK BY WEEK THROUGH THE THEME

FIRST WEEK   ## "CHOOSING THE THINGS WE LIKE"

BOTH SECTIONS   Provide three or four different kinds of things, such as sweets, fruit, toys, pictures, coloured shapes and give the children the opportunity to choose which they like best.

INFORMAL TALK   Ask them why they chose those particular things. Did you choose the dress or jersey you are wearing or whether you had porridge or corn flakes for breakfast this morning?

(The teacher should include some of the choices she has made.)

What would you choose to buy if you had 5p to spend?

Which TV programme do you like best? Why is it your favourite?

Who do you choose to play with at school? Why do you choose to play with him?

Point out that we are always having to choose, but that not all choose the same things; each of us has our favourite colour, fruit, sweets, TV programme and friends.

Ask the children what would have happened if all the children in the group had chosen the same sweet. Point out that we cannot always have first choice, sometimes we must let others choose first.

Note to teachers   The informal talk may provide sufficient material for one week but the additional story is given for those who require it.

GIVING OTHERS FIRST CHOICE

ADDITIONAL
STORY   A very long time ago, long before Jesus was born, there lived in the land of
BOTH SECTIONS   Palestine a man called Abraham. Now Abraham was a very rich man. He had great flocks of sheep and goats and many servants and shepherds to look after them. He did not live in a house as we do. He and his family and all his servants lived in tents and they travelled from one place to another looking for fresh grass for their animals. His nephew Lot had his own flock of sheep and goats and his own servants and shepherds but he always travelled from place to place with his uncle Abraham.

Each day, Abraham's shepherds and Lot's shepherds took their flocks out onto the hills to find fresh grass and in the evening they brought them back to the well where they could get plenty of water.

For a time they were happy together until one day the shepherds began to quarrel.

"Abraham's shepherds take *our* water for their sheep," complained Lot's shepherds. "And Lot's shepherds take *our* grass for their sheep," complained Abraham's shepherds. And so the quarrel went on.

Abraham was worried; he didn't like to hear the shepherds quarrelling. So he called them together. "Let's have no more of this quarrelling," he said. "Let me hear no more of *our* grass and *our* water. God has made the grass and the water for us all to share. Go and get on with your work and stop quarrelling."

But it was no use. The shepherds soon forgot the things Abraham had said and began to quarrel again.

"It's *our* grass; it's *our* water," they shouted at each other.

"There's plenty of land," said Abraham to his nephew Lot. "See how it stretches away to the left and to the right."

"But this part of the country is just not large enough for both of us and our flocks," said Lot. "Our shepherds are always quarrelling with each other."

"Then let us both go to the top of that hill and look at the country round about," suggested Abraham. "We can then choose where each of us will go."

"That's a good idea," agreed Lot.

So they both climbed to the top of the hill.

Now Abraham was the leader of the family and he knew that he could choose first but as he did not want to be selfish he said, "You may have first choice, Lot."

Lot looked around him. On one side he saw rich grass, shady trees and streams of fresh water and on the other side, poor thin grass, hills, rocks and sandy soil. Which do you think he would choose?

"I'll choose that way," he said, pointing to the rich grass, shady trees and streams of fresh water. He was glad Abraham had let him choose first.

A Graph

Before the children leave their class groups to choose an activity, let each child draw his favourite colour, fruit or food on a small piece of paper, 2" x 3". Then during the activities all the children in turn can stick their own drawings on to the paper, already prepared by one of the teachers. Conclusions can be written on the graph.

Our first choice is grapes;
Our second, equal, choice is apples and bananas.

ACTIVITIES

Let the children choose from:

(i) Individual or class books can be made by the children of the food, sweets, clothes and fruit they like. The pictures can be drawn by the children or cut from old magazines and glued into the books.

Alternatively, the pictures could be stuck on a roll of wallpaper to make a poster or frieze.

(ii) A sorting box. Children love to sort buttons, shells, beads, pieces of material, etc. Provide a large box of these articles and invite them to sort out the things they like and put them into egg trays or individual boxes.

(iii) Model making. Various kinds of modelling materials can be provided for the children to make a model of their own choice.

(iv) Dramatisation. Provide a variety of dressing-up materials and let the children act out a story of their choice or dramatise the additional story.

(v) A frieze of the story might be drawn or painted or the children could make a frieze of the things they like.

(vi) Use can be made of the worksheets.

SECOND WEEK

"MAKING CHOICES"

BOTH SECTIONS

Introduction

Ask the children when they have parties. (*Birthdays, Christmas.*)

Have you been to any parties? Do you like going to parties? Why? Point out that when we have a party we usually choose our special friends to come to it. All of us like to be chosen to go to a party. One day Jesus told a story about some people who were invited to a party.

STORY

There was once a very rich man who planned to have a great party. He had many friends, so he chose all the ones he wanted to come to his party and sent out the invitations.

"I am giving a party and I hope you will come," he said. "Yes, thank you," they all replied. "We will come to your party."

Then the rich man called all his servants together and they began to get ready for the party. They cleaned the house, laid the tables, counted the seats and put them in place so that no-one should be left out. The rich man bought the finest food he could buy for his guests.

When everything was ready, he called his servants to him again and said, "Go to the friends I have invited to come to my party and tell them that it's all ready."

But when the servants came to the first house that friend shook his head and said, "I'm too busy to come to the party. I've just bought a field and I must go and look at it. I'm sorry, please excuse me."

The servants came to the next house, and you can imagine how surprised they were when this friend said, "I'm sorry, I cannot come to the party. You see,

I have bought ten goats for my farm and I must go and see them, please excuse me." And away he went to see his ten new goats.

Now when the servants came to the house of the next guest they said, "Surely this friend will come to the party."

But no, he too shook his head and said, "I've just got married, please tell your master that I'm sorry but I can't come to his party. I'm far too busy just now."

And on the servants went. But it was the same at each house, everyone had chosen something else to do and asked to be excused. When they returned to their master and told him that none of his friends could come he was very angry. "What can I do now with all this lovely food that I have prepared?" he wondered.

Then he had a good idea. "We *will* have a party. I will invite other guests. Go quickly into the streets of the town," he told his servants, "and bring in to the feast the poor people who have no homes, the beggars, the lame and the blind."

So the servants hurried out and brought in all those people until every seat was filled. When the rich man saw them all enjoying the good things he had prepared he knew that this was the best kind of party to have.

OLDER SECTION ONLY
Discussion

The people who were invited to the party said, "Yes, they would come" and then they chose to do something else. Was it wrong not to go? Why? (They had promised to go.) Was the man right to invite all the other people afterwards?

ACTIVITIES

Let the children choose from:

(i) A painting, drawing or collage picture of the story. The children should be encouraged to write a short caption under their picture.

(ii) Puppets. Some children might make simple puppets of the characters and then act out the story. (See *Growing Up in the Church—First Year*, pp. 30-31.)

(iii) Dramatisation. The story lends itself to dramatisation as there is plenty of action in it.

(iv) Role playing. A group of children might act out some everyday incidents involving choice.

(v) Choosing games. The children might play games such as "The farmer wants a wife;" "Bee baw babbity" and "I took a letter to my love."

(vi) Use can be made of the worksheets.

D*

THIRD WEEK   **"THE DISCIPLES CHOOSE TO FOLLOW JESUS"**

BOTH SECTIONS   When Jesus began his work there were so many people who needed his
                       help that he asked some men to help him. The men who helped him were
Introduction   called disciples. (*Do you know that word? Let the children say it together.*)

                       Our story tells us about some of these disciples.
STORY
                       One day, when Jesus was down by the seashore he saw the fishermen hard
                       at work. The fish that had been caught earlier that morning had been sold in
                       the market and now some of the fishermen were washing their nets and
                       spreading them out to dry. Others were mending their nets ready for the next
                       day's fishing.

                       Peter and Andrew, two of the fishermen, were standing at the edge of the
                       water throwing their small hand nets out over the water, catching some fish.
                       As Jesus watched them he knew they were just the kind of men he needed to
                       help him.

                       "Peter, Andrew," he said. "Come with me. I need you to help me in my
                       work."

                       Peter and Andrew had already been with Jesus many times. They had
                       listened to his teaching and watched him as he cared for people. But now
                       Jesus was asking them to give up their fishing and help him. What should they
                       choose to do? They loved fishing but it didn't take long for them to choose to
                       leave their boats and go to help Jesus.

                       A little further along the shore, James and his brother John were in their
                       boat helping their father Zebedee. They were helping the other fishermen to
                       mend the nets ready to go out to sea again to catch more fish.

                       "James! John!" Jesus called. "I need you to help me in my work. Come

with me." Like Peter and Andrew they had often been with Jesus as he talked to people and cared for them, so it didn't take them long to choose either. They put down their nets, climbed out of the boat and went with Jesus.

Now Jesus had four fishermen to be his disciples. (*What were their names?* Peter, Andrew, James, John.)

OLDER SECTION ONLY

But Jesus did not ask only fishermen to help him, he also asked a tax-gatherer.

Every day Matthew sat at his table by the side of the road and the people came to pay their tax money to him. Most people didn't like tax-gatherers because they collected money for the Roman Emperor who ruled over their country of Palestine and because they often took more money than they had a right to take.

One day Matthew was sitting at the table when he saw a crowd of people coming along the road. He watched eagerly. He was sure that Jesus was talking to them. As they came nearer Matthew tried to hear what Jesus was saying. Then, suddenly, he was surprised to hear Jesus talking to him.

"Matthew," said Jesus, "I want you to be one of my disciples. Come with me."

Matthew could hardly believe his ears. He had heard what a great teacher and preacher Jesus was and now Jesus was asking *him* to help him. Which should he choose: to help Jesus or to stay a tax-gatherer? Matthew knew that if Jesus needed him he must go with him, so quickly he got up, left everything his money, his books and his pens and went with Jesus.

Before long Jesus had twelve men who had chosen to help him and as they went from place to place with him they learned how to love other people and to care for them as he did.

ACTIVITIES

Let the children choose from:

(i) Painting and drawing. The children could depict the various scenes and write captions under their work. The older children might concentrate on Matthew.

(ii) This story provides a good subject for a collage picture. Teachers should try to provide suitable material for boats, fishing nets and the seashore.

(iii) Modelling. Using a large tray as a base the children could model a seashore scene. Some of the boys might enjoy making boats from scraps of cardboard, string and a piece of material for the single sail. The fishermen could be modelled in plasticine or clay.

(iv) Dramatisation. Both stories could be dramatised more than once to allow all the children wanting to act the opportunity of taking part.

(v) A scrapbook or poster might be made of the drawings or writing done by children who prefer to work on their own.

(vi) The worksheets provide an additional activity.

FOURTH WEEK   **"CHOOSING TO FOLLOW JESUS TODAY"**

BOTH SECTIONS   Ask the children what they would choose to be when they grow up.

STORY

Louisa Cowie wanted to be a nurse. Even when she was quite a little girl she decided that when she grew up she would choose to be a nurse, and as soon as she was old enough she began her training. She had to learn to look after people who had had an accident and people who were ill and had to stay in bed for a long time. She had to learn how to look after mothers and their new-born babies and children who were sick.

When she had finished her training she began her work as a nurse in a big hospital in Scotland. Then one day she heard that in some countries there were many sick people who had no-one to look after them. Louisa Cowie knew that Jesus wanted someone to help these people, so she decided to go and help them.

Now she had to learn about the many different kinds of illnesses that people in other countries have and she had also to learn to speak another language.

At last the great day came when she set sail for southern Yemen. The hospital in Sheikh Othman where she began work was a busy one. Sick people came from the villages round about and many more travelled miles across the desert and over the mountains to get medicine.

OLDER SECTION ONLY

It was very hard work at the hospital. During the hot summer months the sand blew everywhere.

Although Nurse Cowie worked at the hospital most of the time, sometimes she had to make long trips to little village clinics, taking medicine, bandages and ointment to sick people who could not make the journey to the hospital themselves. She travelled in a Land-Rover part of the way and often because the roads were so poor she had to walk the last part or ride on a donkey. As she went she had to watch out for bandits who might be hiding behind the big rocks. But she did not mind how uncomfortable the journey was if she could help the people who were ill to get well again.

Louisa Cowie cared especially for the mothers and the children. It made her sad that the mothers knew so little about caring for their babies. The children had usually been ill for a long time before they were brought to the hospital.

BOTH SECTIONS ACTIVITIES

In the hospital was a tiny brown baby called Amoon. Although Amoon was seven months old she could not sit up like other babies of her age and she never smiled. The time came when her mother grew tired of Amoon being at the hospital and she decided to take her home. As the mother and her baby stayed quite near the hospital, Nurse Cowie visited their home twice a day to see how Amoon was getting on. She saw that the baby got the right kind of milk and medicine until Amoon began to get better again.

Now something more than milk and special medicine was needed if Amoon was to grow into a healthy little girl. But the extra food would cost more money. Where was the money to come from?

One day Nurse Cowie had a letter from some boys and girls in Scotland. "We want to help your little Arab babies," they said. "Here is some money we have collected."

With the money she was able to buy cereal and eggs for Amoon and before long the baby began to make more rapid progress. Amoon's mother took over most of the feeding and care herself and you can imagine how delighted she was when her baby first gave her a big smile. As Nurse Cowie looked at her and her mother she felt glad that she had taught that mother how to look after her baby.

ACTIVITIES

Let the children choose from:

(i) Painting and drawing pictures of the story.

(ii) Dramatisation. Provide nurse sets and dolls for the children to act out the story.

(iii) A model might be made of the hospital. This can be made from a shoe box, beds from matchboxes and patients can be modelled in plasticine or similar modelling material. The boys in particular might enjoy making a Land-Rover from empty cartons.

(iv) Use can be made of the worksheets.

(v) A practical project. The children might collect empty match boxes and cover them with white paper. Small bottles and white linen can also be collected. These should be carefully packed in shoe boxes and sent direct to Church of Scotland Medical Mission, Rada, Yemen Arab Republic.

Scrapbooks containing brightly coloured pictures can also be made and sent to the mission.

The children might be told that their offering this Sunday is going to be used to help boys and girls like Amoon. (This money should be remitted to the Mission and Service Fund by your Church Treasurer.)

7 Praising and thanking God

PREPARING FOR THIS THEME

TIME OF YEAR

This theme is designed to fit into the Primary programme during the month of March.

APPROACH TO THEME

All the things the children do each day contribute to their growth. This theme attempts to bring together worship and their everyday experiences of living. By sharing the experiences of hearing, seeing, tasting, touching, smelling and making the children are led to praise and thank God for them. As we use rightly the powers God has given to us, we show our appreciation of them. The theme develops by showing how all the gifts of Jesus were used "to the glory of God" and how the followers of Jesus today can praise God in their daily work and in all they do. Finally, the children are introduced to two aspects of prayer—thanksgiving and intercession. Prayers of thanksgiving for particular things the children enjoy, fit most naturally into the experience of Primary children. Prayers of intercession for others, especially those whom the children know about in their own experience, give expression to the attitude of compassion and care for others that we wish to encourage.

BIBLICAL FOUNDATIONS

Worthy of praise

Read Ps. 150. God is to be praised for his mighty deeds. We are able to appreciate his creation and his love, and we are capable of giving praise to him. Worship is our response to the nature of God, whom we know through his actions, and we must use the best that we have to offer to express our praise and thanks. Christians have recognised God's love through Jesus Christ, and whatever their circumstances may be they want to praise him. They do so with the whole of their lives. (*See 1 Pet. 1: 3-9.*) We love him, believe in him and "rejoice with unutterable and exalted joy." Our lives should indicate the genuineness of our faith.

Using gifts

Now read Rom. 12: 6. "Having gifts that differ according to the grace given to us, let us use them." The writer speaks of adult gifts which children will not yet have. But children have their own gifts and they can be thankful for them, and be willing to use them.

Read Mark 1: 21-38. In this account of a day in the life of Jesus we see that his gifts are used in the service of others, in teaching, in healing, and in praying for them. His life is lived "to the glory of God."

Aware of God

Look up Matt. 6: 9-15; Luke 11: 1-4. Jesus was able to live like this because he was aware of God's presence and sought his purpose and his strength. Seeing him pray the disciples ask for help. What we say in our prayers is directed by the character of God, our Father, and not simply by our own wants. Jesus is himself our guide to the nature of God.

110

"All of life would become prayer" by Michael Quoist.[1]   *PRAYER*

"If we knew how to listen to God, if we knew
       how to look around us, our whole life would become a prayer,
For it unfolds under God's eyes and no part of it must be
       lived without being freely offered to him.
At first we communicate with God through words
       which may be dispensed with later on.
Words are only a means.
However, the silent prayer which has moved
       beyond words must always spring from everyday life,
       for everyday life is the raw material of prayer."

PRIMARY WORSHIP

A suitable hymn for this theme is "Praise to God for things we see." (See p. 159.)

Other appropriate hymns and songs are—"All creatures of our God and King" (R.C.H. 13); "To God who makes all lovely things" (I.P. 13: 1 and 5); "Sing a glad song" (I.P. 38); "Praise and Thanksgiving let everyone bring" (I.P. 37); "I can praise God all day long" (I.P. 34).

The activities of movement, percussion band and singing as suggested on p. 114 might be incorporated in the closing worship, during this theme. Then when the leader reads Ps. 150 the words will be more meaningful for the children.

The leader might introduce the reading of Ps. 150 by saying, "A long time ago, a man wrote about praising God with all kinds of instruments just as we have been doing. This is what he wrote." Read Ps. 150.

Other Bible readings might include—Ps. 92: 1-4; 1 Cor. 10: 31; Col. 3: 23; Luke 17: 11-16.

THE THEME IN OUTLINE

First week: "Praising God for the things we can do."

This week the children are encouraged to use their senses to explore and make discoveries about the world around them. As they talk informally with their teachers about all the things they can do they are led to praise and thank God for these gifts.

Second week: "Jesus praises God."

The story of Jesus healing the deaf man shows Jesus' care for the deaf. In the story for the older section about a day in Capernaum, we see Jesus praising God in the synagogue and we see the things he did for others. His whole life was lived "to the glory of God."

[1] Reprinted from *Prayers of Life* by Michael Quoist by permission of the publishers, Gill and Macmillan Ltd., Dublin.

Third week: "People in our church who praise God."

People in the church are invited into the Primary to talk about their work. We see that as people use their gifts they can praise God in all they do.

Fourth week: "Learning how to pray."

The story of the leper saying "thank you" reminds the children of the many things for which they should say "thank you" to God. The additional story of Jesus teaching his disciples to pray leads the older children to pray for others.

Suggestions for the Book Corner

Our Book Corner, 3rd shelf, Chambers—"Men and Women at Work" series: *The Miner; The Doctor and the Nurse; The Bus Driver.*

Ladybird books: "People at Work" series: 1. *The Fireman;* 2. *The Policeman;* 12. *The Road Makers;* 13. *The Car Makers.*

I.T.A. "Read About It" series: 8. *The Fishermen;* 12. *The Postman,* by O. B. Gregory (A. Wheaton & Co. Ltd.).

Helping at Home; A Book of Prayers through the Year; The Lord's Prayer (Ladybird).

I open my eyes; This is God's World—Listen!; Smells I like ("Glow-worm Books," Mowbrays).

LEADER'S BOOKS   The leader will find helpful suggestions for the worship in the department in the following books: *Praying with Primaries,* by Dorothy R. Wilton, N.C.E.C. *Please God,* by Beryl Bye and Joyce Badrocke (Falcon).

WEEK BY WEEK THROUGH THE THEME

FIRST WEEK

"PRAISING GOD FOR THE THINGS WE CAN DO"

BOTH SECTIONS IN GROUPS

The teachers should arrange the room before the session begins, setting up various tables or centres with a selection of articles for each group of children to explore with their teacher.

On one table there will be things to see, on another things to touch and on others things to hear, taste, smell and make.

The tables or centres might include some of the following:

Things to see—a vase of flowers, twigs bursting with new leaves, such as catkins, horse chestnut, flowering currant; small, large and coloured shells; pictures of springtime; a mirror; kaleidoscope; magnifying glass; a pair of binoculars.

Things to touch—a holly leaf, pussy willow; pieces of material such as velvet, silk, fur; shells, a smooth pebble, rough rock; a feather; a piece of dough; a saucer of cold water.

Things to smell—an orange, soap, flowers, vinegar, a cut onion, paper, floor polish, chocolate, a moth ball.

Things to taste—nuts, apple, orange, sugar, carrot, salt, sweets, raisins.

The Land-Rover crossing the desert to a village (see page 108).

The town of Sheik Othman.

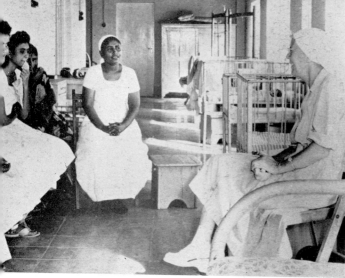

Sister Cowie with the mothers at the hospital (see page 108).

A mother with her family at the hospital.

Amoon and some of the food
that made her well.

Things to hear—a musical box, percussion instruments, such as drum, bells, maraccas; bottles filled with different amounts of water to make an interesting sound when struck with a spoon. Some sounds could be recorded beforehand and then played back on a tape recorder for the children to try to identify (*for example, a man's voice, a woman's voice, a dog barking, a clock chiming, water being poured from one container to another, jingling coins, a telephone ringing, a car horn, a pneumatic drill*). The children might also enjoy recording their own voices and listening to them played back on the tape recorder.

Things to make—using pieces of paper approximately 6″ x 8″, crayons, felt-tipped pens. Cartons of various sizes, brushes, glue, scissors, gummed paper. Flour and salt dough.

The children could see how quickly they could make a simple model or draw a picture.

Suggestions for other things to make can be found in *Play with a Purpose for Under-Sevens*, by E. M. Paterson, Penguin, chapter 9; and in *Making Musical Apparatus and Instruments*, by K. M. Blocksidge, Nursery School Association.

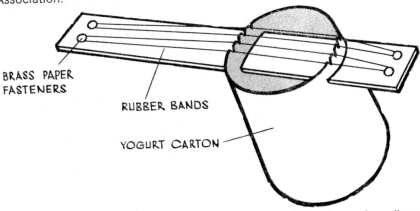

BRASS PAPER
FASTENERS

RUBBER BANDS

YOGURT CARTON

For the guitar you will need a yogurt carton, a thick piece of cardboard 2″ x 10″, 4 brass fasteners and 2 narrow 3″ rubber bands. Cut slits to fix the cardboard, make 4 V cuts on each side of the rim over the slits to hold the "strings" firmly in place.

**BOTH SECTIONS
*Discussion***

Plan for the children to move round in turn to as many of the groups as possible, looking, touching, listening, tasting, smelling and making. The teacher should discuss informally with her group of children at each table or centre the discoveries they make; their likes and dislikes.

When the children return to their own groups they might continue the discussion by talking about other things they can do, such as running, jumping, singing, swimming.

Point out that God has given us all these powers to use and enjoy. Suggest that they say "thank you" to God for each of them.

**OLDER SECTION
*ONLY***

If people who are blind, deaf, or lame have been mentioned in the discussion, then a short prayer of intercession could be incorporated by the teacher.

In Primaries where the arrangements described are not practicable then each teacher should provide a small selection of the articles to use with her own group.

ACTIVITIES

There may not be time for further activities if all these groups are attempted. For those who have time or who wish to extend this session over two weeks, the following activities are suggested:

(i) Movement to music. The children could make up their own dance as they respond to the music played either on the piano or a tape recorder.
The following books would be helpful for the pianist:
60 Melodies for Movement, by Roberts & Gertsman (Bosworth & Co.).
Expressive Movement Themes, by Ruth Carter (Curwen & Sons).

(ii) Percussion band. The children enjoy making music with the percussion instruments; many of these can be improvised. (See *The Church Nursery Group,* p. 23.) They could practise a hymn tune and accompany the singing in the closing worship.

(iii) Singing. Learn to sing, "Praise to God for things we do" (p.159) and the other two verses of this hymn. If the teacher prints the words on a large sheet of paper the children can illustrate it either with their own drawings or with pictures cut from magazines.

(iv) The worksheets provide an additional activity.

SECOND WEEK

**YOUNGER
SECTION**

Introduction

"JESUS PRAISES GOD"

Let the children listen to a watch ticking or tell you some of the sounds they can hear now either in the Primary room or outside in the street. (*Children talking, cars going by, birds singing.*)
Remind them of some of the sounds they heard last week. Ask them what we use to hear all these things. (*Our ears.*) Now ask them to put their hands over their ears very tightly. What can you hear now? Tell the children that there are some people who cannot hear. What name do we give to those who cannot hear. (*The deaf.*)

STORY

In Palestine, the land where Jesus lived, there was a man who was deaf. His ears looked just like other people's ears but there was something wrong inside and so he never heard any sounds at all.
Sometimes the man went down to watch the fishermen catching the fish by the seashore. He could see the waves splashing against the sides of the boat but he could not hear the sounds they made. He could see the children playing out in the street but he could not hear what they were shouting to each other. Because he could not hear he could not speak either.

*Children
participate*

When he went to the shop to buy something to eat or something to wear how would he tell the shopkeeper what he wanted? (*By using his hands, making signs.*) One day some of the deaf man's friends heard that Jesus was in their town, so they took their friend to Jesus.

"Our friend is deaf and he can't speak. Will you help him?" they asked.

Jesus was sorry for the deaf man so he took him to a quiet place away from the crowd of people.

Then Jesus put his hands on the man's ears and tongue and for the first time the man was able to hear and to speak.

What sounds do you think he could hear now? What do you think he would say?

Jesus always helped all those who came to him, the sick, the blind, the lame and the deaf.

OLDER SECTION STORY

Jesus and his disciples were in the town of Capernaum. (*Do you remember the names of any of Jesus' disciples? PETER, ANDREW, JAMES, JOHN, MATTHEW.*)

It was very quiet down by the seashore. There was no fishing going on and the market where the fish was usually sold was empty. It was the Sabbath day, the day of rest and no-one did any work in Capernaum on the Sabbath day. Jesus and his disciples and all the other people went to their church, the synagogue, to sing some of the psalms like the one we heard last week, to pray and to listen to their Bible being read. Today, Jesus was asked to read from the big scroll Bible and all the people were very quiet as they listened to the words he read.

After the service Jesus went to the home of Peter and Andrew, and James and John went with him. Peter's wife's mother hadn't been at the service because she was ill, so they told Jesus about her. He took her by the hand and helped her and soon she was well enough to look after her visitors and prepare the dinner for them.

In the evening, as the first three stars appeared in the sky, the Sabbath day, the day of rest was over. Many people in Capernaum had waited for this time. Now they came along the streets; people who were blind, people who were deaf, people who were lame, and other people carrying their sick friends or relations on their mat beds. It seemed as if the whole town was crowding round the door of Peter's house. They all wanted to see Jesus.

"They must have seen you in the synagogue this morning," said Peter. "And the news of how you help people has spread all over the town."

Jesus healed those who were sick and helped others who were sad. He was always ready to help all who came to him.

ACTIVITIES

(i) TV film. A group of children might make a TV film of the stories. The pictures could be drawn with felt-tipped pens or thick wax crayons and the captions written either by the children or by the teacher. (See p. 141.)

(ii) Painting. Several children could paint the various scenes in the stories (a) Jesus healing the deaf man; (b) Jesus in the synagogue; (c) in Peter's house; (d) the crowd of people coming to see Jesus. The scenes could then be put together to make a frieze.

(iii) Dramatisation. Some children might act out the stories.

(iv) Movement to music, percussion band and singing might be continued today.

(v) Worksheets can be used as an additional activity. A teacher should be available to guide the children who have chosen to work at this activity. The worksheets are not intended for use by the children without some guidance from the teacher.

THIRD WEEK   # "PEOPLE IN OUR CHURCH WHO PRAISE GOD"

Note for teachers   At the preparation class try to arrange for at least two people of the church to visit the Primary this week to talk to the children about the work they do during the week. It is preferable for these visitors to be people who attend the church regularly so that they are known by sight to the children as those who attend the church.

Suitable visitors might include a nurse, a health visitor, a fireman, a "lollipop" man, a teacher, a policeman, a mother, a shopkeeper, milkman, a garage mechanic. (Often young parents are willing to help in this way.)

Anyone who sees his work as service could be invited to help, but those marked out by a uniform may be more interesting for Primary children.

One person can meet the older section and the other the younger section. If more people are willing to help in this way, smaller groups could be arranged, making a much more informal atmosphere in the department.

Arrangements must be made well in advance if this week is to be successful. The Primary leader and some of the teachers should meet with the people beforehand, perhaps inviting them to the preparation class when this theme is discussed, so that they know exactly what is required for this week.

BOTH SECTIONS   Before the visitors go to the various groups play the game, "Who am I?" Make out labels for the visitors.

Ask the visitor to say very briefly what their work is; for example:
    (1) I cook the dinner
        I wash and iron the clothes
        I make the beds and do the shopping
    (2) I stop the traffic
        I see the children safely across the road.

Then let the children guess which label each visitor should wear. In the groups the visitors should introduce themselves by telling their names and something about their families. Then they should tell as briefly as possible something of the work they do. It would make the theme more interesting if the visitors brought along something to show to the children, e.g., a policeman's cap or a nurse's uniform.

Teachers should stay with their class groups and help to guide the discussion.

ALTERNATIVE
PROGRAMME

If people are not available for visiting the Primary the teachers could talk about the work *they* do or role-play the work of various people for the children to guess what each one is doing.

LOOK AT
POSTER

Teachers could discuss the pictures in the books. "People at Work" series, suggested for use in the Book Corner (see p. 112).

ACTIVITIES

(i) Large paintings or collage pictures of the people who visited the Primary today could be made by groups of children.

(ii) Role-playing. Provide suitable props, such as a doctor's set; nurse's uniform; dolls and beds; a policeman's cap or fireman's helmet so that the children can play out the various roles.

(iii) A book for the Book Corner. A group of children might contribute to a class book "People in our Church." Pictures cut from magazines, drawings and writing done by the children can be glued into the book. The cover of the book might be cut out in the shape of the church.

(iv) A poster. The children's drawings and writings could be glued on to a piece of wallpaper or strong brown paper to make a poster. A picture of the church might be used for the centre of the poster.

(v) The children might make a posy of flowers, make a card or write a letter to their mother for Mother's Day.

(vi) The worksheets can be used as an additional activity.

FOURTH WEEK

"LEARNING HOW TO PRAY"

A LEPER SAYS "THANK YOU"

BOTH SECTIONS
Introduction

Ask the children if they have had measles or chickenpox.
What did they look like? (*Covered with spots.*)
Did they have to stay away from school?
Ask them why they had to stay away from school. (*So that no-one else would get it.*)

STORY

Once there were ten men who had to go to live away from their families because they had sores and spots all over them. The men were lepers and so they were not allowed to stay in their village in case other people caught the disease.

One day Jesus was going to Jerusalem. When he was near to the village, he saw the ten men coming to meet him. They had seen Jesus coming along the road that led to the village.

"I'm sure he could help us," said one of them.

"Let's shout," suggested another.

So they shouted as loudly as they could. "Jesus, Master, help us."

Jesus heard their shouting and came towards them and said, "Trust in God. He will heal you. Off you go to the temple in Jerusalem and show yourselves to the priest and you will be well again."

The men hurried off to Jerusalem, praying to be made well again. And sure enough, when they reached Jerusalem all their spots and sores had gone.

The priest in the temple looked at them and said they could go back to their families again now that they were better.

As they were going along the road back to their village, one of the men remembered that Jesus had helped him. So he hurried back to look for Jesus, singing at the top of his voice, praising God for making him well again.

When he found Jesus he knelt down and thanked him over and over again.

Ask the children to suggest some of the things for which they should say "thank you" to God. (*Toys, sweets, homes, friends, food.*) Then together say a prayer of thanksgiving for all these things.

THE DISCIPLES LEARN HOW TO PRAY

AN ADDITIONAL
STORY FOR THE
OLDER SECTION

On another day Jesus had been busy in Capernaum. Ask the children to tell you some of the things Jesus did there. (*Went to the synagogue; healed people who were deaf, blind and lame, made Peter's wife's mother better.*)

Very early the next morning, while it was still dark, Jesus got up and went out of the house to a lonely place. Before long all the people were looking for him. They looked everywhere but could not find him. Then Peter and some of the other disciples saw him.

"He's out on the hillside already," said Peter. "He does like to get away to a quiet place where he can pray, doesn't he?"

"Let's ask him to teach us how to pray when we are with him again," suggested James.

Later that day when the disciples were with Jesus again James said, "We know that you often pray to God. We want to be able to pray, too. Teach us how to pray."

So Jesus taught his disciples the prayer that we say in our church every Sunday.

Ask the children to tell you which prayer it is. Suggest that they say it with you.

Note to teachers

(If the teacher has written out a copy of the Lord's Prayer beforehand, the children can read it with her. They may not know it well but it is enough that they know that Jesus needed to pray and that the disciples wanted to learn how to pray.)

DISCUSSION

Ask the children when we pray. (*In church, in Sunday school, at bedtime, at school.*)

Ask them if they know any prayers. Perhaps they could learn to say a grace or a prayer to say at bedtime.

Let the children suggest those for whom we should pray.

People who are ill; our mother, father and family; people who help others.) (*Remind the children of some of the people they were talking about last week.*) End with a short prayer of intercession, mentioning especially those people whom the children suggested.

ACTIVITIES

(i) Painting and drawings might be made of the stories. The children could write a sentence about their picture or the teacher could write the words the children suggest.

(ii) Dramatisation of the stories. Provide a few clothes, such as old curtains, headsquares and pieces of towelling material for dressing-up, as these will enrich the dramatisation.

(iii) Puppets. The children would enjoy making paper bag or stick puppets, then they could act out the story with their puppets. (See *Growing Up in the Church—First Year*, Introduction, pp. 30-31, and *Second Year*, Introduction, pp. 22-23.)

Wooden spoon puppets. Another kind of puppet can be made from a wooden spoon and a pipe-cleaner. Make a face on the back of the spoon; glue on pieces of string or wool for the hair. Twist a pipe-cleaner round the handle to make arms. (See fig. 1.)

Fig 1.   Fig 2.

Cut a pattern (as in fig. 2) from a piece of material and tie a narrow piece of cord round the waist for a belt. Fix on a piece of material for a head-dress.

(iv) Books to make for the Book Corner. A "thank you" book, using the children's own drawing of the things they want to say "thank you" for and "Our prayers for others" which might include some of the prayers written by the older section.

(v) A prayer card. A short prayer might be printed on pieces of cardboard either by the children themselves or by one of the teachers. These could then be illustrated by the children and used at home each evening for their own prayertime. These should be completed and taken home.

(vi) Worksheets can also be completed and taken home today.

8 Easter

PREPARING FOR THIS THEME

This theme is intended for use during the month in which Easter falls. The material for Palm Sunday should be used on the Sunday before Easter. Wherever possible the Easter service, which is the focal point of this theme, should be held on Easter Sunday, but where local arrangements do not allow this, it can be used on the Sunday after Easter. The material for "Spring" can be used either at the beginning or the end of this theme.

TIME OF YEAR

The most important festival in the Christian Church is Easter, when Christians everywhere celebrate Christ's victory over sin and death and his continuing presence with his Church. As each church is arranging its Easter service it is hoped that the children will be encouraged to share in the worship as part of the church family.

APPROACH TO THEME

The full meaning of Easter and even the Easter stories themselves are difficult for Primary children, therefore this theme tries to ensure that what we teach them about Easter has meaning for them.

In the Easter service, the life, death and resurrection of Jesus are told very briefly as the children participate in worship through story, music and dramatisation.

The theme attempts to help the children to share something of the experience Christians have of joy, hope and new life because Jesus rose on Easter day.

Read Zech. 9: 9-10.
The prophet speaks of the entry of a victorious king into Jerusalem. He comes in peace, riding on a donkey rather than a war-horse. The weapons of war are banished: there is no longer a need for these since the king rules "from sea to sea and from the river to the ends of the earth." The entry of Jesus into Jerusalem before his arrest was his fulfilment of this prophecy. He is prince of peace. (*See Luke 19: 28-38.*)

BIBLICAL FOUNDATIONS
The entry of the king

A king of peace did not satisfy the hopes of the people who wanted a new kingdom to be created by the forcible removal of the Roman invaders. So they turn against Jesus, as he knew they would.

The rejection of the king

Now read John 12: 23-27, 32-33.
Jesus tried to prepare his disciples for his death. It was the completion of one part of his work amongst men, the fulfilment of God's purpose. But it was not the end of all that he was to do; it was the beginning of something new. As the corn of wheat must die to bear much fruit so Jesus must suffer death to give abundant life.

Dying to live

121

The same picture of new life bursting from the seed is used by Paul to illustrate the resurrection. *Look up 1 Cor. 15: 36-38, 42-44, 57.* Because Jesus died and rose again there is available to us this same new life. Because he lives we shall live also. His presence with us opens up for us a new quality of life which our suffering and death cannot take from us. (*See Rom. 8: 31-39.*)

Believing and seeing

Read Luke 24: 13-35.

The presence of Jesus is not always recognised. The travellers to Emmaus do not know him at first though their hearts burn within them as they travel and he interprets the scripture. For them seeing and believing come when Jesus breaks bread for them. They are transformed by the knowledge that he is alive, and they must share the good news with others.

The joy of Easter is the presence of Jesus with us now and for ever. This is the Good News we cannot keep to ourselves. (*See Matt. 28: 18-20.*)

PRIMARY WORSHIP

The hymns suggested for the Easter service will be most appropriate for this theme. It is important to practise the songs for the Easter service so that the children can sing them in a bright and lively way.

Suitable spring songs might be "All the flowers are waking" (I.P. 82); and "The glory of the spring how sweet" (R.C.H. 608 : 1.).

On the first Sunday, the Bible reading might be introduced in the following way. "We all joined in our Palm Sunday procession today, waving our palm branches and shouting 'Hosanna,' now let's hear part of the story of the first Palm Sunday." Read Mark 11 : 7-9.

Other suitable Bible readings: Third week—Matt. 28: 18-20; Fourth week—Song of Solomon 2 : 11-12.

THE THEME IN OUTLINE

First week: Palm Sunday.

The familiar story of "Palm Sunday" is presented in an imaginative way for the younger children, while the story for the other children is read from a modern translation of the Bible within the context of the observance of Palm Sunday in a church in Jamaica.

Second week: An Easter Service.

The Easter service is the focal point of this theme in which the children participate in worship through story, music and dramatisation.

Third week: Jesus is with us always.

The two stories, "Joel Remembers Jesus" for the younger children, and "On the road to Emmaus" for the older children, help them to sense something of the joy and happiness that Jesus' disciples and friends found when they realised that Jesus was alive and with them always.

Fourth week: New life in Springtime.

This week both the stories and the activities help the children to experience something of life, death and new life in the world around them.

Suggestions for the Book Corner

My home in Trinidad (Longman).
What to look for in Spring (Ladybird).
The Farmer (Ladybird).
The Coconut Palm (W. & R. Chambers).
The Blackbird (W. & R. Chambers).
Children who met Jesus (W. & R. Chambers).

Useful background reference books for teachers and children:
The Man who couldn't wait and *Great and Wonderful King* (Arch Books).
Life in New Testament Times (Ladybird).

The story of "A Scottish Blackface Lamb" can be obtained from the British Wool Marketing Board, Educational Department, Oak Mills, Clayton, Bradford, Yorks.

Pictures and samples of wheat for the story of the Lonely Seed (fourth week, younger section) can be obtained from McDougalls Ltd., Wheatsheaf Mills, London, E.12.

WEEK BY WEEK THROUGH THE THEME

PALM SUNDAY

FIRST WEEK

YOUNGER SECTION

STORY

"Hurry up, Joel," shouted Reuben, "or we shall miss seeing Jesus today."

"I'm coming," called Joel.

Joel said "Goodbye" to his mother and ran off down the road with his friend Reuben.

Reuben and Joel had often been with the crowds of people to hear Jesus telling them stories and today they were hoping to see him in Jerusalem.

"There will be crowds of people in Jerusalem," said Reuben. "I'm sure Jesus will be there."

As they hurried along the road they saw two friends of Jesus untying a donkey that was tied to a post in front of one of the houses. Some men said, "What are you doing untying the donkey? What do you want it for?" Reuben and Joel stopped to watch.

"Jesus needs the donkey," said one of Jesus' friends. "But we'll bring it back as soon as he has finished with it."

"Why do you think Jesus wants a donkey?" asked Joel.

"I don't know, but if we follow his friends we'll be sure to find out," suggested Reuben.

And so they followed the two men as they led the donkey along the hot dusty road towards Jerusalem.

"There's Jesus," shouted Reuben as they came near to the city. "He's with some more of his friends."

When the two friends with the donkey reached Jesus, they took off their coats and put them on the donkey's back to make a saddle.

Then Jesus climbed on to the donkey and rode into Jerusalem.

As soon as the people heard that Jesus was coming they ran to meet him. They were so glad to see him that they cut down branches from the palm trees and waved them in the air like flags. What would we do if the Queen came to visit our town? (*Wave flags, put down a carpet for her to walk on.*) This is just what the people in Jerusalem did. Some of them even took off their coats and spread them on the ground like a carpet so that Jesus could ride over them like a king. And all the people shouted "Hosanna! Hosanna in the highest! Hosanna!" Reuben and Joel joined in, too. They got some palm branches and waved and shouted "Hosanna!" as loudly as they could.

"That was a great procession," said Reuben.

And neither of them could stop talking about it when they got back home that night.

OLDER SECTION

STORY

"PALM SUNDAY IN JAMAICA"

Ask the children if they know what this Sunday is called. (*Palm Sunday.*) Tell the children that in some countries the people celebrate Palm Sunday by having a procession. They wave palm branches and shout "Hosanna!" just as the people did in Jerusalem on the first Palm Sunday. We celebrate Palm Sunday in our church, too, but I'm going to tell you about Benjie, a little boy in Jamaica and the Palm Sunday service in his church.

The little church on the top of the hill was decorated with palm branches.

There were palm branches on the Communion table, palm branches on the pulpit and even the front door had two huge palm branches over it.

On Palm Sunday, all the children stayed in the church with the grown-ups for the whole service. Benjie, dressed in his newly-pressed black trousers, clean white shirt and black bow tie, sat very still. It was a hot day, all the doors and windows of the church were wide open and Benjie could see the mountains and the big, tall palm trees without even turning his head.

The seats in the church were hard but Benjie tried to sit still. He knew Grandma in her lovely white straw hat with the bright red flowers was watching him and she would be mad with him afterwards if he misbehaved. Benjie stood up straight and sang the hymns with the grown-ups. He closed his eyes and bowed his head for the prayers. Then when the minister read from the Bible, Benjie listened all the time.

It was the same story as we heard in our church this morning. Let's listen to it again.

"Jerusalem was in sight. Jesus sent his friends to a village. 'Go into the village,' Jesus said, 'and just as you go in you'll find a donkey. It'll be tied up. Untie it and bring it; and if anyone asks you why you are doing this, tell them: 'The Master needs it,' and he'll send it to me.'

They went off, and found the donkey tied at a door outside in the street. They untied it.

'What are you untying the donkey for?' asked some of the people standing by.

They said what Jesus had told them to say, and the men let them take it away.

They brought the donkey to Jesus and threw their clothes on its back. Jesus sat on it. People spread their clothes on the road, and others cut palm branches and spread them out. All the crowd, those in front and those behind, shouted,

'Hurrah!

Happy is he who comes in God's name!

Happy is the Kingdom of King David, our father!

A thousand times—Hurrah!' "[1]

Benjie was very interested in the story.

He knew all about donkeys, he rode one often. Nearly everybody I know rides on a donkey, thought Benjie. I'm glad Jesus rode on one.

Benjie also knew about the palm branches. He was glad Jesus knew about palm branches, too.

These palm branches look lovely. They should be in church every Sunday, he thought.

In the sermon Benjie heard the minister telling the people that Jesus was King and that was why the people waved palm branches in Jerusalem on the first Palm Sunday. They were waving them like flags and cheering to welcome Jesus as a King.

As the service ended all the children joined in a procession waving palm branches and shouting "Hosanna!" Benjie joined in, too, and made his "Hosannas" the loudest of them all.

[1] Mark 11:1-11. Adapted from *New World* by Alan T. Dale, by permission of the Clarendon Press, Oxford.

ACTIVITIES

FOLD

CUT

Give the children a choice from the following activities.

(i) A hobby-donkey and palm branches. A group of children could help to make a hobby-donkey and palm branches ready for the dramatisation on Easter Day. (See *Growing Up in the Church—First Year*, p. 77, for instructions for making a hobby-donkey.)

A simple way of making palm branches would be for the children to tie green crepe paper to a twig. Alternatively, they might paint or draw large palm leaves and cut them out or fold a piece of paper 9" x 12" and cut as in diagram. The leaves can then be glued to pieces of cardboard approximately 1½" wide by 15" long.

(ii) Dramatisation. Let the children act out the story either of the first Palm Sunday or of Palm Sunday in Jamaica. Broom or laurel can be used to represent palm branches if the children do not make their own. The children might like to make a procession around the room and shout "Hosanna."

(iii) A spring garden could be started ready for use later in the theme. Plant some grass seeds in earth on a large tray. If small paste pots or shaving foam tops are placed at intervals in the earth, fresh spring flowers can be put into these on Easter Day.

(iv) Singing. A group of children might enjoy practising the hymns ready for the Easter service.

(v) Worksheets. Use can be made of the worksheets but this should always be an additional activity.

PREPARATION FOR THE EASTER SERVICE

Some preparation is necessary if the Easter service is to run smoothly. Dressing-up materials and any props required need to be ready in advance. Six children from the older groups or six teachers are required as narrators. The words should be printed on a card for the children to take home to practise. There is no need for them to learn them by heart but the service will be helped if the words are read well. The leaders should retain duplicate copies of the words ready for use at the service. Suggest that the children help to make the room attractive for Easter day by bringing some spring flowers.

SECOND WEEK

AN EASTER SERVICE FOR PRIMARY CHILDREN

BOTH SECTIONS
Preparation for the service

Before the service begins, the teachers should try to prepare the room with vases of spring flowers and leaves. It is assumed that the Primary service will be carried out in the room where the Primary usually meets.

The first part of the time should be given to preparing the service and the second part to the service itself.

All the children in the Primary should be involved in the service in some way, either as narrators or in the dramatisation of the various scenes. In large Sunday schools where there are too many children for all to be involved in the dramatisation, a choir group could be responsible for the singing. There are six main groups for the dramatisation and these can either be the usual class groups or groups specially arranged for the occasion. A larger number of children is required for the crowd in scene 4 and children who have already acted in other scenes might be included in this scene also. Scenes 5 and 6 are more appropriate for the older children to dramatise.

In the groups the following steps might help the preparation of the scene.   ***In the groups***

(i) Recall the story or scene and discuss the various people in the story.

(ii) Let the children choose the part they want to play and discuss how they will act the story. The children can mime or use their own words for the acting. If they choose to mime, the teacher in charge of the group should outline the story as the dramatisation takes place. This allows the other groups to know exactly what is happening in the service.

(iii) Let the children choose their own dressing-up clothes and help each other to dress up. Allow time for each group to practise the scene before meeting together.

(iv) The narrators also need time to practise their readings.

When the groups are ready, arrange the chairs in a semi-circle, leaving plenty of space in the centre for the various scenes to be dramatised. It is better that the dramatisation takes place in the "round" like this than on a stage; it allows the service to be an act of worship rather than a performance.

The Easter service should proceed with the minimum of interference and direction from the teachers.

AN EASTER SERVICE

Music: Play part of the "Hallelujah Chorus" or "Jesus Christ is risen today." (Use a record player or tape recorder.)

Leader: Jesus Christ is risen today.

All: Hallelujah! Hallelujah!

All sing: "Christ is Risen, Hallelujah!" (see p. 163).

Narrator 1: In our Easter service, we shall remember the story of Jesus from the time he was born in Bethlehem until the first Easter day. We begin our story as the wise men visit him bringing their presents of gold, frankincense and myrrh.

Scene 1— Dramatisation of wise men bringing their gifts.

All sing: "Still the Night" (R.C.H. 49 : 1).

Narrator 2: When Jesus began his work there were so many people who needed his help that he asked some men to help him. As the disciples went with Jesus, they learned how to love other people and to care for them as he did.

Scene 2—   Dramatisation of Jesus asking the disciples to help him.

All sing: "In Galilee beside the sea" (I.P. 69).
Narrator 3:   Many people came to Jesus, the blind, the deaf, the lepers, the lonely and the sad. He helped all who came to him. He healed the sick and was a friend to those who were sad and lonely.

Scene 3—   Dramatisation of Jesus helping many people. (The healing of the ten lepers might be included here.)

All sing: "Jesus' hands were kind hands" (I.P. 70 : 1).
Narrator 4:   On the first Palm Sunday, Jesus rode into Jerusalem on a donkey. The people waved palm branches and shouted "Hosanna" to welcome him like a king. But the enemies of Jesus planned to kill him.

Scene 4—   Dramatisation of the entry into Jerusalem.

All sing: "Children of Jerusalem" (R.C.H. 658 : 1) or "Christ is coming" (see p. 163).
Narrator 5:   One night, when Jesus went into a garden to pray, his enemies caught him and on Good Friday they put him to death. The disciples were afraid and ran away.

Scene 5—   Dramatisation of Jesus being arrested and the disciples running away.

All sing: "There is a green hill far away" (R.C.H. 105).
Narrator 6:   On the Sunday morning, one of the women who had been a friend of Jesus, ran to tell the disciples that Jesus had risen from the dead. At first they could hardly believe it. But later, when Jesus came and said to them, "I am with you always," they knew it was true.
                 Jesus was alive.

Scene 6—   Dramatisation of the woman telling the disciples the Good News.

All sing: "Easter Day brings joy and gladness" (see *Growing Up in the Church—1st Year,* p. 144, *2nd Year,* p. 148.)
Prayer: O God, we thank you for Jesus who was born in Bethlehem,
(Taken by   for his work of healing those who were sick and for helping all
leader)   those who needed him. On this Easter day, we are glad when we remember that Jesus is alive and with us always. Amen.
All sing: "Christ is risen, Hallelujah !"
Music: Play Easter music again.

JESUS IS WITH US ALWAYS

"JOEL REMEMBERS JESUS"

"Mother! Mother!" called Joel.

"I'm up here, Joel," called his mother. "What is it? Why are you so excited?"

Joel hurried up the steps that led to the roof and rushed across the flat roof to his mother, who was busy spreading grapes to dry in the sun.

"Oh, mother! Is it true? Is it?" he asked.

"Is what true, Joel?" asked mother. "What's wrong, son?"

"Reuben and I were thirsty and we went to the well for a drink, and the women there said we wouldn't see Jesus any more," Joel said.

"Yes, it's true. We won't see Jesus, but . . ." said Joel's mother.

"But why, mother?" interrupted Joel. "Jesus is our friend. Why won't we see him? And yet the women seemed so glad! Why are they glad if they won't see Jesus any more?"

"Let's sit down and talk. I can finish spreading the fruit to dry later," said mother.

"We all loved Jesus very much because of the kind things he did to help people, didn't we?"

"He helped me make a boat once when he stayed at our home," said Joel.

"Yes, he did," smiled mother. "You both had a good time. He was always glad when the children came to see him. He liked to hear them sing. And do you remember how he helped sick people?"

"He helped a blind man, didn't he, mother?" asked Joel.

"Yes, he helped many people," she said.

E

"People liked him so much they had a big proces-proces . . ." Joel stumbled over the big word.

"Procession ? Is that what you are trying to say ?" smiled mother.

"Yes. Procession ! I went to Jerusalem with Reuben, didn't I ? Jesus rode on a donkey and people waved palm branches and sang, 'Hosanna !'" said Joel.

"Yes. They all sang, 'Hosanna ! Hosanna !'" added mother. "Jesus and his helpers were very glad on that day, but some people in Jerusalem didn't like some of the things Jesus said and did, so they hurt him so much that Jesus died. That is why we will not see him again."

"But why aren't you sad, mother ?" asked Joel, very slowly.

"Well, son, God loves us so much that he made a wonderful thing happen. He made Jesus live again in a very special way. Some of his friends have seen him. This is good news for all of us. We are glad that Jesus lives, even though he will not come to visit us as he used to do. But he will always be with us." [1]

"ON THE ROAD TO EMMAUS"

OLDER SECTION
STORY

There was once a man called Cleopas and he had been in Jerusalem with his friend for the great feast of the Passover. They had been among the crowd who had welcomed Jesus as their King as he rode into Jerusalem on a donkey. Do you remember how everyone had been so glad to see Jesus on that day? Later, they had seen the enemies of Jesus capture him and put him to death. Now as Cleopas and his friend walked slowly home to the place called Emmaus they were sad and puzzled. All they could think of was what had happened in Jerusalem during these last few days.

"If only every day could have been like that day when we all waved palm branches and shouted 'Hosanna !'," said Cleopas.

"Yes," said his friend, "it's hard to believe that the enemies of Jesus hated him so much that they killed him."

"One of the women told the disciples this morning that Jesus is alive and she had seen him, but I can't believe that, can you ?" asked Cleopas.

While the two friends were talking, another traveller joined them and walked along the road with them.

"Why are you sad ?" he asked. "What has happened ?"

"Don't you know ?" asked Cleopas. "If you don't then you must be the only visitor in this part of the country who doesn't. I thought everyone knew."

"Tell me about it, I should like to know," said the traveller.

And so they told him all about Jesus. How he had healed the sick and helped many people. They told him how the people had welcomed him into Jerusalem and how his enemies had captured him and put him to death.

"That is why we are sad," said Cleopas. "We shall never see our friend again."

"One of the women who knew Jesus came to tell the disciples only this morning that he is alive and she had seen him," said his friend. "But we can hardly believe that."

At first the traveller listened. Then he talked to them. He told them not to be sad and that although Jesus had died that was not the end of the story.

---

[1] Adapted from *Helping One Another* by Christina J. Owen, a Kindergarten Course Book in the United Church Curriculum .Copyright 1962, United Church Press. Used by permission.

It was so interesting that the time passed quickly and almost before they knew it they had reached Emmaus.

The traveller was going to walk even further on, but Cleopas said, "It's getting late, come in and stay the night with us."

So he went in with them. Then as they all sat down to have supper, the stranger took the bread in his hands and broke it and gave it to them.

"It's Jesus. That's just as he used to do," thought Cleopas and his friend. And it was Jesus. He was alive, as the woman had said.

Later, when Jesus was with his disciples again he said to them, "I will be with you always."

PREPARATION FOR NEXT SUNDAY

Before the children leave their class groups to work at the activities, let them help to plant beans or peas in a jam jar with wet blotting paper and sawdust. (The beans or peas can be fixed to the blotting paper with a small piece of sellotape.) If these are soaked well they should be sprouting by next Sunday. The children will then be able to see the shoots and the roots of the seeds which will be helpful when they hear the story about the seeds next week.

ACTIVITIES

Give the children a choice from the following activities:

(i) Painting, drawing or collage pictures can be made of the stories either by individual children or a group of children working together on a frieze.

(ii) A scrapbook could be made for use in the Book Corner. This can include writing and drawings about Easter. The older children might like to imagine they are Cleopas writing about the journey to Emmaus.

(iii) Model. A model of Joel's house could be made. A shoe box might be used as the house with matchboxes glued together for the steps leading up to the rooftop. The outside of the house might be covered with "polyfilla" to give a rough stone effect.

Figures could be made either from pipe-cleaners or clothes-pegs and added to the model.

(iv) Dramatisation. Both of the stories could be acted out. As only a few characters are required for each story, they might be acted out more than once to allow more children to take part.

(v) Use can be made of the worksheets.

E*

NEW LIFE IN SPRINGTIME

"THE LONELY SEED"

**YOUNGER
SECTION**

STORY

A farmer had some corn seeds (*if possible show some corn seeds or a picture of some*) and he wanted them to grow into new corn stalks with more seeds to make into flour for bread. He ploughed his field to make the earth soft and then he put the seeds into a seed box.

"You're all going to be planted in the earth today," he said.

"Oh, but we don't want to," they cried. "We shall be spoiled; our golden brown coats will get wet and dirty!" But there wasn't anything they could do about it. The farmer carried them off to the field in his seed box.

As they were going, one seed which was a bit bigger than the others said, "Don't let's be too sad. The farmer knows what is best for us. Just think we shall grow into new green plants and we shall forget all about our golden brown coats!"

But there was one seed who was determined not to be planted! He slid to the bottom of the box and tucked himself in one of the cracks.

"I'm not going to be planted in the earth. I'm not going to have my golden brown coat spoiled. How do I know whether I shall grow a new green shoot?" And he squeezed himself still further down into the crack.

The farmer went up and down the field with his tractor, scattering the seeds till they were all gone—all, that is, except the one that hid. He was stuck in his safe little hole and there he stayed.

"Ha! Ha!" he chuckled. "That was clever of me! I'm safe."

After a while the farmer went out to work in his field.

The rain had fallen and the sun had been shining and where he had planted the seeds there were now beautiful, fresh green shoots showing against the brown earth.

"How splendid they all look in their new green coats," he said. The corn plants stretched up tall, feeling very proud of themselves. They had forgotten about their golden brown coats in the earth which were now dirty and finished with, and were enjoying the sunshine.

But what about the seed that hid? What had happened to him? Nothing! He was still all by himself in the little crack at the bottom of the seed box. He had no green coat. He could not feel the rain and the sun and he never heard the farmer say, "How splendid" to him. He was a very lonely little seed and quite useless!

When the autumn came the seeds in the fields had grown tall and strong and had turned a lovely golden brown. On the top of each stalk was an ear of golden brown seeds—lots of them! (*Show an ear of wheat or a picture of one.*)

(Story from *Alive in God's World*, First Series, Book One, by the Wadderton Group (Church Information Office).

"THE LOVELY PEACH"

There was once a peach growing on a tree in a garden. As the roots of the tree sucked up the moisture in the ground, the peach began to swell with juice. The warm sunshine glowed on its velvety skin and it ripened to a beautiful pink, tinged with streaks of gold and crimson. (*Look at a peach or a picture of one.*)

One day someone came and picked the peach. It was taken into the house and laid on a dish for all to see. People admired it and said it was the most beautiful one they had ever seen.

But the time came when it was so perfectly ripe and juicy that it was ready to be eaten. That was a sad day for the peach. First the velvety skin was peeled back and then it felt teeth biting into it. "What a lovely taste," said a voice. And soon nothing was left of it but the hard woody stone inside, which was thrown out of the window, where it landed with a bump on the soil in the garden. There it became dry and dirty and was lost and forgotten. (*Show a peach stone.*)

Nobody wanted the peach now. Sometimes a spade or a garden fork knocked against it, and it was pushed about, but it gradually became completely buried under the dark soil.

In the winter the ground froze hard, but in the spring the sun melted the frost and soft warm rain fell on the earth above the peach stone and trickled down. Soon it felt strange and as the soil became warmer it was surprised to discover that its hard, woody shell had cracked open.

Inside the shell was a large seed which had swelled in the warm moist earth until it burst open and sent out a shoot. Part of the shoot grew down and sent out roots and part of it grew up and up, until above the ground came two tiny green leaves on a little stem.

As the months went by it went on growing. The roots reached down further into the soil for more and more food washed down by the rain, while the sunshine drew up the stem until it became sturdy and strong. It grew more leaves and little branches until it became a tiny tree.

In the autumn it dropped its leaves and in winter it rested. Then one glorious spring day the little tree had another surprise. Where there had been little hard brown bumps on its twigs, fat little buds peeped out, which soon grew into lovely pink blossoms.

"How pretty," said the people passing by. "Look at this little peach tree in full bloom. Wherever did it come from?"

The little peach tree smiled to itself.

That summer, where the flowers had blossomed, three ripe peaches grew on the branches.

"I had to die first, before I could live again," thought the little peach tree.[1]

Give the children a choice from the following activities:

(i) Wonder table. Prominence should be given to the wonder table and all the children should be encouraged to look at and talk about the things on it. With the materials you provide try to make a contrast between winter and

---

[1] Adapted from a story by Constance W. Stark.

spring, things that look dead in winter and their new life in spring. (*Bare twigs with tight buds and twigs with many new leaves; a packet of seeds and seeds growing, planted earlier by the children; a hyacinth bulb and a flowering hyacinth.*)

Look at beans or peas planted last week.

Some children might make a poster of pictures cut from magazines of lambs, flowers and animals, to display behind the wonder table.

(ii) A "looking walk" could be arranged to a park or garden. This group might look and listen for signs of new life in spring. (*Flowers growing, birds singing and building their nests.*) They could write about the things they saw when they return.

(iii) Growing things. A group of children might plant some flower seeds in the church garden or in the model garden planted earlier in this theme. They could watch them grow during the next few weeks.

(iv) Dramatisation. The children might enjoy making up a spring dance. They could be bulbs, trees, birds. The bulbs could curl up and sleep in the ground. The rain falls, the sun shines and they grow up and up, spreading out their arms until the bulb is flowering. The pianist could play suitable music or pre-record with a tape recorder music from various sources such as "Morning" from *Peer Gynt Suite.* The dance could be included in the closing worship.

(v) Painting, drawing or collage pictures could be made. Encourage the children to make a contrast between winter and spring. (*One picture can show bare trees, brown earth in winter and another the new life in spring, new leaves, birds building nests, new lambs.*)

(vi) Use can be made of the worksheets.

9 Helping others

PREPARING FOR THIS THEME

This theme is intended for use after the Easter theme. It is most suitable for the month of May when it can be conveniently linked with the Church's Christian Aid project.

TIME OF YEAR

The theme begins by helping the children to recognise the importance of their hands which enable them to work, help and play and leads them to thank God for their health and strength. Jesus is the focal point in every theme in this Primary programme and in this theme we see how his love and compassion for people in need helps them to live their lives to the full.

The theme develops by showing how the Christians in the early Church continued the work of Jesus when he was no longer with them, by helping people in need. Christians should always feel concerned in a world so full of need.

The Church today continues the work of Jesus as it serves the community and we must help the children to share in the Church's ministry of helping and caring for others.

Finally, the children are involved in practical projects which are within their capabilities and understanding, and as they participate they are led to realise that they are helping to carry on the work of Jesus today.

APPROACH TO THEME

Read John 10: 7-11. Jesus is the good shepherd and cares about his flock just as God is the Shepherd of his people and looks after them (e.g., Ps. 23). He wants what is best for us and came to give us life in its fullness. God's purpose is not to restrict our lives or to diminish us (as many of the Jews insisting on the strict observance of the law seemed to want) but to set us free to live as "children of our Father who is in heaven." The motive of Christian behaviour is the love which characterises God's family and which is shown completely in Jesus himself. This quality of life is intended for us all.

BIBLICAL FOUNDATIONS
Life abundant

Read John 4: 45-54. John sees the healing of the nobleman's son as a sign of the rule of God present in Jesus. He came to bring health of body, mind, and spirit. Jesus always responded to the needs of people, refusing to work miracles on demand as proof of his authority, but willingly bringing to those in need the healing which they sought.

Signs of the Kingdom

Look at Matt. 12: 9-13 and Luke 6: 6-10. Jesus shows that the well-being of people takes precedence over the keeping of the Sabbath. The Sabbath itself was designed for our good and certainly ought not to hinder our compassion for others. We are to love the Lord our God with all our heart and mind and strength *and* our neighbour as ourselves. Indeed "he who does not love his brother whom he has seen cannot love God whom he has not seen." (1 John 4: 20.)

The rule of love

Love in action   See Acts 11: 27-30. This concern of Jesus for others was taken up by the first Christians and from the beginning it has been characteristic of the followers of Jesus. As we receive the love of God in Jesus we are to respond by our concern for others. We accept responsibility for those who are in need and we help in any way open to us whatever that need may be.

USEFUL   Useful photographs and leaflets about people in need can be obtained from
INFORMATION   the following organisations:
The Save the Children Fund, 29 Queen Anne's Gate, London, S.W.1;
United Nations Children's Fund, 58 Royal Exchange Square, Glasgow, C.2;
Christian Aid, Scottish Office, George IV Bridge, Edinburgh.
    With this material teachers can make their own posters for this theme, but should *avoid using distressing pictures with young children.*

PRIMARY WORSHIP

Suitable hymns for this theme might be: "Hands to work and feet to run" (I.P. 45); "For all the strength we have" (I.P. 31); "Jesus' hands were kind hands" (I.P. 70, alternative tune—*Au Claire de la lune*); "Praise to God for things we do" (p. 159); "This is the way we use our hands" (tune—Mulberry Bush); "God has given us work to do" (I.P. 44).
To introduce the Bible reading for the third week, the leader might say, "Once when Jesus was speaking to his disciples he said, 'I say to you, as much as you did it to one of the least of these my brethren, you did it to me.' (Matt. 25: 40.) He was telling them that as they fed those who were hungry, gave a drink to those who were thirsty and clothes to those who hadn't any it was as if they were doing it for him.
Other Bible readings—Col. 3: 23; John 15: 12.

THE THEME IN OUTLINE

First week: Using our hands.
    This informal talk encourages the children to talk about all the things they are able to do with their hands and leads them to think of ways of using their hands to help others.

Second week: Jesus helps others.
    In the story of the healing of the rich man's son for the younger children and the healing of the workman for the older children, we see Jesus' compassion for those in need and his readiness to meet that need.

Third week: The Christians in Antioch help others.
    This week's story attempts to show how the Christians in the early Church tried to continue Jesus' ministry of love, by helping people in need.

Fourth week: The Church helps others today.
    In these stories the children are led to think of the needs of others and to see how people today help and care for others as Jesus did. In the projects that follow the children are given the opportunity of becoming involved in giving to others.

Suggestions for the Book Corner

"Men and Women at Work" series from "Our Book Corner," 3rd shelf (W. & R. Chambers Ltd.).

The Roadmakers; The Builder; The Nurse; The Shipbuilder; Helping at Home; Play With Us; Things we do; Things to Make; Toys and Games to Make; Jesus the Helper (Ladybird).

WEEK BY WEEK THROUGH THE THEME

USING OUR HANDS

FIRST WEEK
BOTH SECTIONS
INFORMAL TALK

Ask the children to tell how they have used their hands since they got up this morning. (*Dressed, washed, ate their breakfast.*)

Ask what other things they can do with their hands. (*Paint, draw, play, help, carry, write, look after their pets.*)

GAMES TO PLAY
Using our hands

(i) *A miming game:* "What am I doing with my hands?" Let the children act in turn and the others guess what they are doing. (*Putting on my coat, cleaning my teeth.*)

(ii) *A guessing game:* Provide some objects such as a comb, a book, a key, a pine cone, a pencil, a marble. Ask the children to close their eyes and use only their hands to feel what the objects are or alternatively put the objects in a bag and let the children feel what is inside.

(iii) *Skills using only one hand* (older groups only) : Let the children try out various skills using only one hand (e.g., tying a shoe lace or ribbon ; building a tower with "lego" or blocks ; fastening a button).

(iv) *Giving commands:* The teacher might show how hands can sometimes be used instead of speaking (e.g., come to me ; sit down ; stand up ; be quiet ; go over there).

HANDS THAT
WORK

Discuss with the children how mother and father use their hands. (*Cooking, shopping, working, lifting.*)

Point out that hands are important for looking after the family and for working to earn money to buy food and clothes.

Lead on to all the various kinds of work that people need strong hands and arms to do. (*Building houses, making roads, driving buses and lorries, working in shops, typing letters.*)

HANDS THAT HELP

Talk about the people who use their hands to help others, the doctors and nurses, farmers, dentists, fishermen.

Ask how we can all use our hands to help others at home, at school and in the church.

Point out that we enjoy doing all these things, playing, working and helping, because we are healthy and strong. God has given us strong arms and legs and healthy bodies to enable us to do these things and we should thank him for them.

End with a short prayer of thanksgiving for all the things we can do with our hands. The teacher should try to include in the prayer some of the things which have been discussed by the children.

ACTIVITIES

Give the children a choice from some of the following:

(i) Finger painting. This week lends itself to this kind of activity. Finger paints can be bought or made from a mixture of cold water paste and powder colour. For this activity aprons and good hand-washing facilities are essential. The children could make a picture of their own choice or just experiment with the materials.

(ii) A large poster entitled "We use our hands" might be made. Let the children either draw round their hands and cut out for the centre of the poster, or make hand prints. Then they can either cut out pictures from magazines or draw their own pictures of people using their hands to glue round the edge of the poster.

(iii) Role playing. Provide various house corner materials, such as dolls, cup and saucer, dressing-up materials and let the children play out various roles (e.g., the mother looking after the family; the father going to work).

(iv) Games. The children might play some games which involve the use of their hands (e.g., fuzzy felt pictures; "lego"; jig saw puzzles and constructional screwing toys).

(v) Model making. Provide scraps of wood, a hammer, saw and nails, or some junk materials, cardboard, cartons, scraps of cloth, glue and string and let the children make a model of their own choice. Clay or a home-made dough might also be used for making models.

(vi) "My Book about Helping Others." For children who like to work alone, provide materials for making a book about this theme. They can add a page each week. This week they can draw a picture and write about using their hands. A group scrapbook might be made in a similar way.

(vii) Worksheets provide an additional activity.

JESUS HELPS OTHERS

"JESUS HEALS A LITTLE BOY"

SECOND WEEK

YOUNGER SECTION STORY

In the town of Capernaum on the shores of the lake of Galilee lived a little boy with his father and mother. He lived in a fine house, not far from the seashore, with plenty of servants to look after him. His father was a very rich man.

Every day the little boy liked to go to play with his friends. Sometimes they played games out on the hillside and sometimes they played down by the seashore, watching the fishermen bringing in their catch or mending their nets. "Perhaps one day I'll be a fisherman, too," he thought.

Then, one morning when he woke up his head was very hot and his arms and legs were tired. He didn't want any breakfast, he didn't want to get up to play; he just wanted to lie still on his bed.

"Come and play," called his friends.

"But I don't want to play," he said to his mother. "My head aches and I'm much too tired."

His mother looked after him all day.

"Perhaps you'll feel better again tomorrow," she said.

But the little boy didn't get any better and everyone was very sad.

His father heard that Jesus was in the town not far away. He had heard how Jesus had made many sick people well again so he said, "I'll go and find Jesus and ask him to come and make my little boy well again. I'm sure he will."

So he got on his horse and away he rode as fast as he could until he found Jesus.

"My little son is very ill and I'm afraid he will die," he said. "Please come quickly and make him well again. I know you can."

"Go home," said Jesus. "Your son will live."

So the father set off home knowing that Jesus had made his son better.

E**

When he was nearly home, some of his servants came to meet him. "Your son is well again," they shouted, and as they hurried to the house together the father told them all that had happened.

When they came to the house the boy ran out to meet them.

"Look, I'm better, I'm better," he shouted. "Now I can run and jump. Watch me."

And he ran off to play with his friends.

OLDER SECTION   "JESUS HEALS A WORKMAN"

STORY   Ask the children to tell of the things they did last week in the Sunday school. (Point out that most of them are strong and healthy and can do all these things.)

In the land of Palestine, where Jesus lived, there was a man who worked very hard. He was a stonemason. Every day he cracked big heavy rocks with his heavy hammer and chisel until they were just the right size and shape for building a house. He needed a lot of stones to build a house and when he had chiselled enough, he built them up one on top of the other until the house was finished. Sometimes there were houses that needed repairing and he helped to put them in order again. Sometimes the shepherds out on the hillsides needed new sheepfolds to keep their sheep safe at night and he helped to build them. It was always hard work and he needed his strong hands and arms to hammer and lift the big heavy boulders.

Then, one day, as the stonemason was busy working there was an accident. One of the big stones fell on his hand and it was badly injured. It was the hand he used most and now he could not use it at all. The sore healed quickly but his

arm would not move, it just hung useless by his side. He could not do his work any more. He needed two strong hands for that. Whenever he saw the other workmen busy doing their work, he wished that his arm was better and he could work again.

One Sabbath day, when the workman went to the synagogue in Capernaum, Jesus was there speaking to the people. (*Explain briefly that Saturday was the Sabbath day, the day when the people in Palestine went to the synagogue to worship God.*) The workman had heard a lot about Jesus. He knew he was a friend of the fishermen, Peter and Andrew. He had heard how he had healed many people who were sick. Even his friend who had been a leper had been healed by Jesus.

"If only Jesus would make my hand better," he thought as he looked at his useless hand hanging by his side, "then I could do my work again."

Suddenly, when Jesus had finished speaking to all the people, the workman was surprised to hear Jesus speaking *to him.*

"Get up and come to me," Jesus said. All the people in the synagogue turned to look at the workman.

Some of the Jewish leaders were angry when they saw what was happening. They didn't like Jesus healing on the Sabbath day. (*Explain briefly that the commandment said they should not work on the Sabbath day.*)

But Jesus turned to them and said, "What is the right thing to do on the Sabbath day? Make someone better or let him die?"

"Stretch out your hand," he said to the workman.

"How can I do that?" thought the man. "I haven't been able to move my arm for months."

But because Jesus had asked him, he tried to move it. To his surprise he found that he could stretch it out as Jesus had said and it was as strong as the other one.

"Thank you, thank you," he said. "Now I have two strong hands, I can work again."

ACTIVITIES

(i) A frieze. The children might paint or draw the scenes of the stories either as a group activity or individually. Let the children suggest captions for their pictures.

(ii) Dramatisation. Provide some dressing-up material for the dramatisation of the stories. The teacher should discuss the action of the stories with the group before they begin to act them out.

(iii) A TV film might be made of the stories. The pictures can be drawn with brightly coloured felt-tipped pens and the captions written under the pictures. The TV can be made from a large cardboard carton. Cut out the space for the pictures, fix two pieces of dowelling as in the diagram. Attach the pictures to a length of kitchen or wallpaper with glue. Fix the ends of the length of kitchen or wallpaper to the dowelling with strong drawing pins.

(iv) Puppets. A simple puppet can be made by using a "ski" yogurt carton for the body and glueing either an old table tennis ball or a ball of paper on the top for the head. Clothes can be made from scraps of material or wallpaper. The features can be made from scraps of felt or buttons stuck on with a strong glue, such as "Gloy Multiglue."

Make a hole in the base of the yogurt carton in order to fix the puppet to a stick (approximately 12″ long). The story can then be acted out with the puppets.

(v) "My Book about Helping Others" might be continued and a picture of Jesus helping others could be added.

(vi) Some of the other activities introduced last week might be continued.

(vii) Worksheets provide an additional activity.

THIRD WEEK

THE CHRISTIANS IN ANTIOCH
HELP OTHERS

BOTH SECTIONS

STORY

After Jesus had died, some of his followers who were called Christians, tried to carry on his work. Some of them taught, some preached, others helped and cared for people.

Paul and Barnabas, two of the followers of Jesus, went on long journeys to other towns and cities to tell as many people as they could about Jesus.

Wherever they went some of the people they met became followers of Jesus, too. Because they had no special buildings in which to worship, they had to meet in one another's houses to talk about Jesus and to remember the things he said and did. Sometimes they met in the early morning before they went to work and sometimes late at night when it was quite dark. Very often they met to have a meal together. Everyone brought some food with them and all shared the meal. Some of the people even sold their land and their houses so they could help people who needed food and clothes. Soon there were groups of Christians meeting like this in Jerusalem and Antioch and in many other towns and cities.

One year, in the country around Jerusalem the crops didn't grow and there was very little food for the people in Jerusalem. Even the little food there was, was very dear. The Christians were often hungry because even those who had been rich had used their money to help the poor and now they had no money left to buy food.

"What shall we do?" they said. "Where can we get help?"

Then Agabus remembered that in Antioch, a town a long way away from Jerusalem, there were some Christians who might be able to help them.

"They are followers of Jesus too," he said. "Surely they will help others who are in trouble. It's a long journey to Antioch, but I will go and ask if they will help us." So off he went.

When he reached Antioch he met Paul and Barnabas.

"The Christians in Jerusalem are hungry," he told them. "The crops haven't grown and there is hardly any food and the people haven't any money left to buy the little food there is. Is there anything you can do to help them?"

"We must not let them go hungry," said Paul. "Christians must always be ready to help people."

The Christians in Antioch said, "Yes, we must do something to help these friends in Jerusalem. We will collect as much money as we can and Paul and Barnabas can take our gifts to Jerusalem for us."

During the next few days, the Christians in Antioch collected some money, then Paul and Barnabas set off with it to Jerusalem. The journey took several days and they had to keep a sharp look-out for robbers.

When they reached Jerusalem they called together all the Christians and said, "We have brought this money from the Christians in Antioch. They were sorry to hear you were hungry and they wanted to help you."

This was great news. Now they could buy enough food, and no-one needed to go hungry.

ACTIVITIES

Give the children a choice from the following:

(i) Painting or drawing. The children might draw or paint pictures depicting the various scenes in the story.

(ii) Dramatisation. Discuss the story with the children and then let them act it out in their own way.

(iii) "My Book about Helping Others." This might be continued and a picture of one of the scenes in the story included.

(iv) Projects. Since more than one week is required for the projects suggested for the fourth week (see p. 146), these can be introduced today, preferably to a group of children.

(v) Use can be made of the worksheets.

THE CHURCH HELPS OTHERS TODAY

FOURTH WEEK

Note to teachers

Find out beforehand what facilities there are in the area for children to play, especially if the children in your class live in high flats. If there are no play facilities for them, perhaps the local church could be the instigators of a playgroup.

YOUNGER SECTION

Introduction

Ask the children where they play; with whom they play and the games they play. Ask them if they have seen high flats. Point out that many children who live in high storey flats like these have nowhere safe to play and often no-one with whom to play.

(In Primaries where most of the children live in high storey flats this introduction can be modified.)

STORY

"You're making far too much noise, Diana," said Mother. "Find a nice quiet game to play or Mr. and Mrs. Gray will be complaining again."

But Diana didn't really want to be quiet. She wanted some of her friends in to play. Diana is four and a half and not quite old enough to go to school like you. She lives with her Mummy and Daddy and two big brothers, right at the top of a huge block of flats. Mr. and Mrs. Gray who live in the flat below are very old and often complain if Diana has her friends in to play and they make a noise. Then the man who lives next door goes to work at night and sleeps during the day, so Diana has to be quiet so that she does not wake him. At the weekends Daddy takes the family into the park to play. Diana likes that because she can run and jump and shout as much as she likes, but during the week she only goes out when she goes shopping with her mother.

One morning when Diana and her mother were shopping they met Mrs. Reid. "Hello," said Mrs. Reid. "Hello," said Diana. "Where are Brian and Sally today?"

"They're at the playgroup," said Mrs. Reid. "I'm just going to fetch them home for dinner."

"What's a playgroup?" asked Diana.

"Come with me and see," said Mrs. Reid.

So Diana and her Mummy went with Mrs. Reid to collect Brian and Sally.

"Eeeoww!" yelled Brian and some of the other boys and girls at the playgroup. They were playing cowboys and Indians.

"Would Diana like to come to the playgroup every day?" asked one of the ladies in charge.

"Can I, Mummy?" asked Diana. "I should like to play at cowboys and Indians with the other boys and girls."

"And do lots of other things, too," said Mrs. Reid.

"Of course you can come," said Mummy. "I shall be glad for you to have some friends to play with."

Now Diana goes to the playgroup every day. She is growing strong and healthy and she is happy because she can play with other boys and girls.

Explain to the children that running a playgroup like this is one of the ways the Church cares for boys and girls.

(The information about Diana and Chang was supplied by "Save the Children Fund".)

OLDER SECTION — THE CHURCH HELPS OTHERS TODAY

Introduction

Do you remember the story of Jesus healing the workman and the story of the Christians in Antioch helping the people in Jerusalem? Recall the stories very briefly.

STORY

The Church today tries to carry on Jesus' work by helping others.

In the country of South Korea, not far from China but a very long way from Scotland, lives Mrs. Kim and her six children. Their house is one little room made of wood, tin and cardboard and their only money is a few pence a week that Mrs. Kim earns by doing washing and other odd jobs.

"Now you children, be good, because I've got to go and do this washing. Don't fight; play quietly together," said Mrs. Kim. Then she walked slowly down the rough mountain road to the little stream with a bundle of washing on her back. Quickly she began to wash the big bundle of clothes in the stream. Mrs. Kim hasn't a washing machine or even any hot water to do the washing.

The five older children went out to play at football and soon they disappeared down the hill out of sight.

"Wait for me. Take me with you. Take me, too," called Chang as he tried to follow them.

Chang is the baby of the family. He is three years old and small for his age because he has never had enough to eat.

As he ran after the older children he did not see the fire where his mother had prepared the rice for their dinner and he fell right into it.

His mother heard his screams and ran as fast as she could up the hill and back to the house. When she saw Chang's hands she knew that she must get him to a doctor as soon as she could. But a visit to the doctor in Korea costs money and Mrs. Kim hadn't a penny in her purse. What could she do?

Fortunately Mrs. Yan, one of her neighbours, lent her five pence so she could take Chang to the doctor.

The doctor gave him an injection but he said, "You must take Chang to the big hospital where he can stay until he is well again."

"But I have had to borrow five pence already," said Mrs. Kim, "I just haven't any money to take him to hospital."

"Then I can help you," said the doctor. "Some people who live a long way from here in the country of Scotland collected money and sent it to help children like Chang."

And so Chang was able to go to the big hospital. Now he is well and strong again and he can run about and play with other boys and girls.

DISCUSSION BOTH SECTIONS

Discuss with the children ways in which your church helps to look after people in need in your own parish and community.

Mention could be made of visitation of sick and elderly by the minister, elders and others; the distribution of flowers and fruit especially at harvest time; playgroups; Children's Homes; Homes for old people; hospitals; collecting for Guide Dogs for the Blind.

Point out that this is how Jesus' work of healing and caring for people is carried on today.

OLDER SECTION ONLY

Discuss with the children how people in need in other countries are cared for by the Church through Christian Aid, Save the Children Fund and United Nations Children Fund.

AT THE PREPARATION CLASS

A collecting box might be made by fixing a paper plate to a strong carton. This could then be used for uplifting the offering today. If a number of boxes are made some children might like to take one home and collect one penny each meal for a week. The money could then be sent to Christian Aid, Save the Children Fund or U.N.I.C.E.F.

**PROJECTS
BOTH SECTIONS**

Before the children leave their class group to work on the projects, discuss the projects with them and point out that they are helping and caring for others as they make and give their gifts.

With the project work it is essential that each child in the group is given the opportunity of making a contribution to the project as a whole. Teachers should make sure that all the children know where the gifts are going.

One or more of these projects should be attempted.

**YOUNGER
SECTION**

1. *A Surprise Box* of toys and games to give to a child who has been ill for a long time or who is in hospital. The children could include in the box a scrapbook (made from pictures cut from birthday cards or magazines) ; a pencil box can be made from a date box covered with attractive paper or fablon ; toys and games they have made themselves. (See Ladybird books, *Things to Make; Toys and Games to Make.*) They might also like to include some toys or games of their own as gifts for this box.

2. If enough things are made for this surprise box it could be given to a playgroup or the children's wards of a local hospital or a Children's Home. A playgroup leader, a nurse or housemother could be asked to visit the Sunday school to receive the gifts or a small group of children could deliver them. One or two of the older children might write a letter or make a card to be sent with the gifts.

3. The children might bring gifts of flowers, fruit or sweets to give to the sick or elderly people in the community. They could help to make the flowers into posies, using a cake doily and silver paper ; and the fruit into baskets of fruit, using papier mache trays and covering with cellophane paper. A group or individual card could be made to be delivered with the gifts. Arrange for groups of children and their teachers to distribute the gifts as part of the activity.

OLDER SECTION

1. This group might organise a stall of goods *they* could sell to parents and church members and the money could be sent to Christian Aid.

(*a*) The children could save some of their own sweets each week or they could make some with their teacher. (See recipes, *Growing Up in the Church— Second Year,* Theme 2.) The stall might also include other things the children have made or gifts they have brought.

(*b*) The children could write cards inviting parents and church members to buy the things from their stall.

(*c*) Let small groups of children be responsible for arranging the stall and selling the goods.

2. Making a poster. Some children can make posters telling of the work of Christian Aid, e.g., your 5p will buy a pen, rubber and pencil for a school boy or girl ; 9p will buy milk for one child for one week ; 50p will buy a blanket ; £5 will buy a cot and mattress for a sick child. Further information can be obtained from the address on page 136.

3. A box of sweets, fruits and flowers for an Old People's Home or Geriatric Ward in a local hospital. Let the children help to make up posies of flowers and pack the box with the sweets and fruit. If it can be arranged, the children could visit the Home or the ward to deliver their gifts. A group or individual card might be made to be delivered with the gifts.

10 A summer theme

PREPARING FOR THIS THEME

This summer theme is designed to operate during the month of June. The Promotion and Flower service comes as the climax of this session and where Sunday schools do not continue to the end of June this service might be used at the end of the May theme.

TIME OF YEAR

Praise to God for the continuing activity of his love is the heart of this theme. God cares for us and shares our joy and we develop fully as we respond to the rich environment which he has provided for us. Part of our environment is the company of others around us who are equally loved by God and in our relationships with them there is an opportunity for the growth of our own personality.

In the Primary programme the church is helping the children to respond to God's love in ways appropriate to them so that they will grow towards Christian maturity.

APPROACH TO THEME

Read Ps. 95: 1-7.
The psalm begins with a hymn of praise to God for his goodness and his greatness. He is the Creator and rules over nature. (Look at Job 38-39 and Isa. 40: 6-31. These are further magnificent words expressing the glory of the Creator and his gracious dealings with man.) The greatness and goodness of God is seen even more clearly than in creation when we consider his relationship with people. He is the "Maker" of his people who are his special care. They are of value because he is interested in them.

The praise is followed by an appeal to Israel to fulfil her obligations, and this is an integral part of the psalm. Those who know God recognise his majesty, rejoice in the love he has shown and respond to him. People who worship God must also obey him. Then they are his people and are "of his making."

BIBLICAL FOUNDATIONS
Rejoicing in God's Creation

Read John 6: 1-13.
We do not study this passage as an illustration of the miraculous. Our concern is the sharing together of the crowd in the experience of being with Jesus, of following him with enthusiasm, and in particular to notice the willingness of the boy to share what provisions he had, however small they seemed. His resources are available for others through Jesus.

There is here in embryo the kind of fellow feeling which is expressed later in the more complete sharing which we find at the beginning of the Church's life (*Acts 4: 32-35*). This kind of sharing may no longer be possible, but the spirit of it is to be expected when we respond to the generosity of God's love in Christ.

Sharing with each other

Read Eph. 4: 11-16.
We all have differing gifts which we may use for the benefit of the whole community—for the building up of the body of Christ. The aim of our growth is stated to be "the unity of the faith and the knowledge of the Son of God."

Growing up in Christ

147

When this happens the Church will have attained "mature manhood" and "the measure of the stature of the fullness of Christ." The Church is viewed not as individuals working towards their own ends but as a single body growing towards full strength. But if this is to be so the individual must be willing to share with others what he has received, to grow towards maturity in Christ.

In 2 Thess. 1 : 3, the writer gives thanks because the Thessalonians are growing abundantly and the love of every one of them for one another is increasing. We, too, should rejoice as the children in our care grow in the grace and knowledge of our Lord and Saviour, Jesus Christ.

PRIMARY WORSHIP

The hymn for the theme might be : "Let us sing our song of praise" (Hymns for Younger Children) (H.Y.C.).

Other hymns might be—"All things bright and beautiful" (I.P. 1. Alternative Tune) ; "God who made the earth" (R.C.H. 20: 1-4) ; "For all the strength we have" (I.P. 31 and H.Y.C. 2) ; "For the beauty of the earth" (I.P. 4) ; "God who put the stars in space" (I.P. 6) ; "Thank You" (see p. 162).

The children, with the help of a teacher, could write their own verses for a hymn. Words that rhyme are not important at this stage. The tune for "Let us sing our song of praise" or "Thank you" might be used.

The first week the leader might introduce the Bible reading in the following way. "In the filmstrip, John and Mary saw many things at the seaside. Here are two verses from the Bible that tell us about the sea."

Read Ps. 95 : 5a ; Ps. 104 : 25.

Other appropriate Bible readings are Ps. 74 : 16-17 ; Gen. 1 : 31a ; Ps. 104 : 24 ; Luke 2 : 52.

Prayers: Wherever possible the prayers of thanksgiving the children have helped to write during this theme should be used.

Music to listen to: Use a record or if a record player is not available, pre-record some music on a tape recorder for the children to listen to either as an activity or during the worship time. Suitable music for this theme would be—"Summer" from "The Four Seasons" by Vivaldi ; "Fingal's Cave" from "The Hebrides" by Mendelssohn.

THE THEME IN OUTLINE

First week: "We enjoy the summer."

By use of the filmstrip or the story about the things John and Mary do during their summer holidays, the children are encouraged to talk about all the things they enjoy doing in the summer.

Second week: "Sharing a picnic."

The children's experiences of picnics and of sharing are used as the context for this biblical story of sharing told from the point of view of the boy who shared his lunch.

Third week: "Sharing a holiday."

All children enjoy visits to the seaside, picnics and holidays. In this story they see how a holiday at the seaside is shared with others.

Fourth week: "We are growing up in the Church."

Finally, a discussion about growing up at home and in school leads the children to discuss their growing up within the church family and helps them to understand their place within it.

Suggestions for the Book Corner

What to Look for in Summer; The Seashore and Seashore Life; The Weather; The Night Sky; Happy Holiday (Ladybird).
All Things Bright and Beautiful (Mowbrays).
The Boy who gave his lunch away (Arch Books).

WEEK BY WEEK THROUGH THE THEME
"WE ENJOY THE SUMMER"

FIRST WEEK

BOTH SECTIONS

Introduction

Ask the children what time of year this is. (*Summer.*)

Ask them what they like best about summer. (*Playing out-of-doors, the longer days, the sunshine, holidays from school.*)

Ask them what they like to do in the summer. (*Play in the park; go for picnics into the country or to the seaside; go for a holiday.*)

Note to teachers

(Some children in your group may never go away on holiday or for a picnic. Where this is so, avoid stressing these aspects and concentrate more on playing with friends in the park or on the back green.)

FILMSTRIP
Note to teachers

(The filmstrip "This Wonderful World" can be obtained from National Christian Education Council, Robert Denholm House, Nutfield, Redhill, Surrey; or Religious Films Ltd., 6 Eaton Gate, London, S.W.1, who also supplied the commentary printed below.)

In Primaries where it is not possible to use the filmstrip, the commentary for the filmstrip can be used as a story. If teachers feel that there is too much material in the filmstrip for one week, Frames 1-8 can be used the first week and Frames 9-15 the following week.

In the filmstrip/story we are going to see/hear about John and Mary on holiday at the seaside. John and Mary are twins and they are just about as old as you.

FILMSTRIP OR STORY

Frame 1—"I wish the train would hurry up," said John, as he hopped up and down the platform. "I'm glad we are going off to the seaside for a week," said Mother. "We need a holiday." Mary hugged her new book. "I hope it will be warm enough to go on the beach. I want to look for some of the shells in my book."

Frame 2—Mary and John woke early on the first morning of their holiday and rushed to the window. "It's a wonderful day. The sun's shining," they cried. "Let's go and paddle in the sea." Quickly they found their bathing costumes and ran down to the beach. "Ooh, it's cold," called Mary, as she splashed in the shallow water.

Frame 3—Digging a sand-castle made John feel warm. Mary dipped her toes into a rock pool. "This is much warmer than the sea," she said. "Mind you don't slip on the rocks," warned Mother. "The thread seaweed makes them very slippery."

Frame 4—There were lots of things to do on the beach. Mary looked into the pool. "It's a good job I didn't keep my toes in the water for long," she said. "Just look at those crabs. They might have nipped my toes." Round the edge of the pools were shells. "There're lots of limpet shells—just like the ones in my book," said Mary. "I shall take some back to school for our nature table."

Frame 5—John took a long green piece of seaweed back to the house where they were staying. "My teacher says that some country people put a piece of seaweed on their door post, so that they can tell when there's rain in the air," he said. "On a fine day it's stiff, but when the seaweed goes limp they say it's going to rain." "It's a good job we brought our wellington boots and anoraks," said Mary. "Let's hope the seaweed will be stiff tomorrow and that it will be sunny again."

Frame 6—"Put on your cardigans this morning," said Mother, when she woke the twins next day. "The wind's blowing hard." It was a good day for drying the swimming towels and costumes. "The breeze will dry the clothes quickly." Father bought a kite for John. "Come on," he said. "Let's see how the wind helps us to make it fly." Mary made herself a windmill. "I like windy days," she said. "My windmill goes round very fast when the wind blows."

Frame 7—The sea, which had been bright blue on the first day of the holiday, now looked grey and rough. "No wonder the radio announcer warned shipping of the high winds," said Father. "Look at that rocket," cried John. "That's a flare from a ship in trouble," explained Father. "The lifeboat is going to help." "I'd like to be a lifeboat man when I grow up," said John.

Frame 8—"You would learn a lot about the weather if you were a lifeboat man," said Father. Mary remembered something. "My teacher told us about some of the things which give an idea of what the weather is going to do," she said. "Let's look for a flower called the scarlet pimpernel—if it is closed in the morning, it's a sign of rain." "Some people say that the cows sit down when it's going to rain," said John. "It's fun to look for the different signs of weather. Perhaps I could be the man on television who tells you what the weather is going to be like."

Frame 9—"Look at the clouds," said John, as the twins went out for a walk with Ruff, the dog owned by their landlady. "They look different when the weather is different. There're lots of wonders to see in the sky." "Do you remember the wet day we had on Monday?" asked Mary. "The sky was grey. We were glad of our wellington boots and poor Ruff got very wet. It looks as if it may rain again today."

Frame 10—The clouds grew heavier and darker as the afternoon went on. "It's a good thing we took Ruff for his walk early," said John, as he knelt on the settee and looked out of the window. "Can you hear the thunder?" asked Mary. "I've put my hands over my ears, but I can still hear it." "That last flash of lightning lit up the room. It's a proper storm."

Frame 11—Next morning the sky was bright again. "The black clouds have gone away," said Mary. "Those white clouds look too thin to hold any rain. It's a day for my tee-shirt, not for my anorak," she cried, as she danced at the top of the cliff. "The sky looks lovely today. Those clouds are called cirrus clouds," said Mother. "Don't they make a pretty pattern in the blue sky?"

Frame 12—"I like the sky at night," said John, when the twins went to bed. "Look at the twinkling stars and the silver moon." "Can you see the big star Daddy calls the Pole Star?" asked Mary. "I don't know which one he means," answered John.

Frame 13—"Look in the book he gave you," said Mary patiently. "Daddy said that you can see the Little Bear with the Pole Star at one end of it." "I like the names of the stars, the Great Bear, the Little Bear, the Milky Way. I wonder who chose their names?" asked John.

Frame 14—At breakfast time, Father had a plan for the day. "We have had lots of different sorts of weather this week. I thought we might go to the weather station, where they keep the records of the wind and the sun." The children put on their slacks and anoraks. "It will be cold on the roof of the weather buildings," said Father. When they got there, Mary looked at the wind gauge, while Father showed John the temperature recorder. "The wind gauge must have turned round very fast on Monday, when we dried our swimming things," said Mary.

Frame 15—"We saw lightning and the Little Bear stars, as well as white clouds and black clouds." "I shall make a night-time picture for my book," said John. "I've got some dark blue paper to make a lovely dark sky and I shall stick a white moon on it."

"What a lot of things I must write down in my nature book this week," said Mary, when they got home.

ACTIVITIES

Let the children choose from the following:

(i) Modelling. A model of a seaside or park. Many of the children might be interested in making a model and this can be continued throughout this theme. Different children might choose to help each week.

Boats, swings, roundabouts, deck chairs can be made from empty cartons of various shapes and sizes or from plasticine or play-doh. Blue paper can be used for the water and green paper or green towelling material for the grass. The sand can be made by pasting glue on to a strong sheet of cardboard and covering it with sand or from a sheet of sandpaper. The people can be made from pipe-cleaners or clothes-pegs. (See *Growing Up in the Church—First Year*, p. 28.)

The teacher should discuss the model with the children before they begin and let them suggest how to arrange the scene.

(ii) A frieze. Using crayons, paints or collage materials a group of children might make a frieze of a seaside or the park as a background for the model.

Provide materials also for individual paintings or collage pictures.

(iii) Out-of-doors. If the weather is suitable, arrange for a group of children to play out-of-doors with balls, skipping ropes, kites, either in the park or in a garden. They could write about their play when they return and this might be used in the worship time.

(iv) A night-time picture. Three sheets of paper are needed, one white and one dark blue, of equal size, and one black sheet which should be the same length but half the width of the other sheets. Use a stiff knitting needle to pierce holes in the dark blue paper, to give the effect of stars, when this sheet is stuck on the white one.

Use a scrap of white paper to make a moon. The black sheet will form a street at night silhouette.

Draw the shape of chimneys and roofs along the upper edge, cut out and stick on the blue paper.

(v) A scrapbook. Drawings, poems and prayers about all the things we enjoy in the summer time might be included in a scrapbook. Poems like "There are big waves" by Eleanor Farjeon might also be included. The children will enjoy drawing the illustrations.

> "There are big waves and little waves,
> Green waves and blue,
> Waves you can jump over,
> Waves you can dive thro',
> Waves that rise up
> Like a great waterwall,
> Waves that swell softly
> And don't break at all,
> Waves that can whisper,
> Waves that can roar,
> And tiny waves that run at you
> Running on the shore."

(From "Come Follow Me" by Eleanor Farjeon from *Poems for the Young and Very Young*, Evans Bros. Ltd., by permission of David Higham Associates Ltd.)

(vi) The wonder table. A group of children might set up a display of the things which interest them. It might include various kinds of shells, a piece of seaweed, a sea urchin, pebbles from the beach, summer flowers. The children should be asked to bring materials for this display.

(vii) Worksheets can be used as an additional activity.

"SHARING A PICNIC"

SECOND WEEK

Note to teachers

Most Sunday schools arrange a picnic for the children but if a picnic has not been planned try to arrange to take your class group into the park to play some games or to visit the seaside or a farm. This can be arranged either for a Saturday afternoon or for a weeknight. In either case take a picnic with you.

In Primary departments where the children never go for a picnic try to arrange to take them for one *before* this Sunday.

BOTH SECTIONS
Introduction

Ask the children if they enjoy going for a picnic. Have they a favourite spot for a picnic?

Discuss the picnic you had or are planning to have.

Today we are going to hear about a boy who went for a picnic. This is a story we can read in the Bible.

STORY

A long time ago in Palestine, the land where Jesus lived, a boy (let's call him Dan) asked his mother if he could have some food for a picnic. He wanted to go off for a long walk among the hills around the Sea of Galilee. Dan was quite a bit older than you so his mother said, "Yes, but don't go too far and remember to be home in time for supper." After his mother had prepared the food for him he set off into the warm sunshine.

Dan had been walking for some time when all at once he was surprised to find a crowd of people who were listening to someone speaking to them. Suddenly he realised this must be Jesus, the great teacher and healer he had heard his mother and father speaking about. This was a chance to see Jesus himself and to hear what he had to say. So Dan gradually edged his way through until he was right up to the front of the crowd.

But something seemed to be wrong. Jesus and his disciples were looking worried. Dan wondered what could be the matter. What were they saying? "Master, these people have been out on the hillside for many hours, they must be hungry. We have no food and not nearly enough money to buy food to feed all these people," said one of Jesus' disciples.

"Please, sir," said Dan. "I have five barley loaves and two small fishes, I shall be glad to let you have them."

"Thank you very much. I shall give this to Jesus," said Andrew, one of Jesus' disciples.

Now when Jesus was given Dan's picnic he turned and gave Dan a smile, then he said to his disciples, "Ask all the people to sit down." When Jesus had said "Thank you" to God for the food the disciples shared it among the people. And there was more than enough for everyone.

ACTIVITIES

Let the children choose from the following:

(i) The model of the seaside or park can be continued today. Figures of people having a picnic might be added.

(ii) Painting, drawing, or collage pictures might be made of a picnic the children have enjoyed and of Dan's picnic. The pictures should then be displayed side by side.

(iii) Dramatisation. Let the children act out (*a*) getting ready for a picnic; (*b*) going for a picnic, and then follow on with the acting out of the story about Dan's picnic.

Some cups and saucers, orange juice, biscuits and sandwiches might be provided for the children to have a picnic although they will enjoy a pretend picnic just as much.

(iv) Writing. Some children might like to write the story as if they were Dan telling another child of his exciting day. These stories could be included in the scrapbook.

(v) The scrapbook could be continued, adding stories and drawings about the picnic.

(vi) The display on the wonder table can also be continued.

(vii) Worksheets can be used as an additional activity.

THIRD WEEK

"SHARING A HOLIDAY"

BOTH SECTIONS

Introduction

Are you looking forward to your school holidays? What kind of things will you do?

I'm going to tell you about Bobby and Jenny and what happened in their school holidays.

STORY

Bobby and Jenny lived in a very old house right in the middle of a big city. Tall buildings, almost black with soot and dirt, towered high above them. There was no garden to play in and no lovely parks near at hand. The sun hardly ever shone in their street and the houses were dull and dingy. Yet Bobby and Jenny were happy children, full of fun and full of mischief.

They enjoyed school. Best of all they loved painting and playing games in the playground.

The school holidays were here again and some of their friends were going on holiday to the seaside. Bobby and Jenny had never been to the seaside or away from home for a holiday at all. "What would it be like there?" they wondered. They wished they might go there some day, too.

Then, one day, when they were playing, Mummy called to them. "Come here, I want you to meet Mrs. Jones."

Bobby and Jenny had never seen Mrs. Jones before but they had often heard their Mummy talking about her.

"How would you like to go to the seaside with Mrs. Jones?" Mummy asked. The seaside! The children could hardly believe their ears!

Almost before they knew what was happening Mummy had them ready to go with Mrs. Jones in her car. They were so excited they could hardly speak. Into the car and away they went. There, at last, was the sea and the glorious sand that was lovely to race along, make sandcastles with, and run your fingers through. What a time the children had! Mrs. Jones had two children of her own and the four soon became friends.

The day passed quickly and it was time to say "Goodbye" to their new friends. When they reached home there was Mummy at the door to meet them. It was lovely to see her again. And they told her all about their wonderful day at the seaside. They had been there at last.

Note to Teachers

(For children who either live by the sea or are used to long holidays and picnics by the sea, the following ending might be added.)

Additional ending for story

Fancy never having been to the seaside! Can you imagine that? But there really are many children who have never seen the sea. You might have the opportunity one day of taking someone to the seaside for the very first time, and if you do I am sure you will enjoy it too.

ACTIVITIES

Let the children choose from:

(i) A TV film. Using the children's drawings and paintings make a TV film about Bobby and Jenny.

(ii) A collage picture of the four children at the seaside might be made, using shells, seaweed, etc. Include all the things they might have seen and enjoyed.

(iii) Dramatisation. Let the children act out the story, playing the various roles.

(iv) Painting. The children might paint different incidents in the story and join all together to make a frieze with captions written either by the children or by the teacher.

(v) The model, wonder table and scrapbook can be continued today.

(vi) Writing. Some children might like to write the story as if they were Bobby or Jenny at the seaside.

(vii) Writing a hymn. Using the tune "Let us sing our song of praise" or "Thank you" a group of children, with the help of a teacher, might write some words for a hymn. This can be included in the service next Sunday.

"WE ARE GROWING UP IN THE CHURCH"
A PROMOTION AND FLOWER SERVICE

Note to Teachers

In many Sunday schools this is Promotion Sunday, therefore there is much activity in the department and a great deal of excitement among the children.

It is a Sunday when some children are saying "Goodbye" to the Primary department and feeling quite grown-up in their new status of being Juniors. These children may be taken to be introduced to their new department and its leader and shown their new place of meeting.

There may be another group, this time from the Nursery to be introduced to the Primary. Therefore there must be a very individual and personal approach to this Sunday, one which will suit the situation in your church.

BOTH SECTIONS INFORMAL TALK

Encourage the children to talk about some of the things that have happened during the year.

Growing up at home

Remind them of some of the interesting things that have happened at home. (*John's new baby brother; Ann's new pet rabbit; Billy's visit to his uncle's farm.*)

Point out how much they have grown during the year. (If there is a wall measure in the Primary Department (see *Growing up in the Church—Second Year*, Theme 1) then the children can measure themselves to see how much they have grown.)

Growing up at school

There will be other signs of their "growing up" (*new front teeth, larger shoes, last year's summer clothes too small this year; things they can do for themselves, e.g., dressing, tying shoe laces*).

Ask them what they have learned to do at school. (Most of the children in the younger group will have begun to read and write. The older children will probably be writing their own stories.)

Encourage them to tell of any interesting projects they have done at school.

Growing up in the Church

Discuss some of the things that have been made by the children during the year. (*Models, puppets, friezes, the new table cloth for the worship centre.*) The people who visited the Primary and the stories the children have heard can be recalled in this way.

Discuss the fact that the older children are going into the Juniors and new children are coming into the Primary from the Nursery. (Some of the children may have older brothers and sisters going into Seniors or the Bible class, others a younger member of the family who will be joining the Nursery group.)

Point out that we are all growing up in the church.

PROMOTION

Allow time for the oldest Primary children to go, with their teacher, to meet their new leader and teacher in the Junior room. The Nursery leader should also bring the group of Nursery children into the Primary to meet their new teacher and to see the Primary room. Both groups will return to their own room for the closing worship.

Some children can help to prepare the flowers, fruit and cards ready to distribute to the sick after the service. Others can help to prepare the room for the service. (Friezes and models made during the theme should be displayed.)

"THANK YOU, GOD, FOR EVERYTHING"　　　　　　　　*SERVICE*

Music:	Play part of "Summer" from *The Four Seasons* by Vivaldi, or part of *Fingal's Cave* from the *Hebrides* Overture by Mendelssohn.
Hymn:	"Let us sing our song of praise" (I.P. 84).
Look at:	Let the children bring forward the friezes and models they have made about the summer.
A Poem:	Some children might read a poem about the summer.

This poem was written by a child for the "Thank You" service in her Primary.

> "I love the hills,
> To climb a tree,
> I love the hills because they're high;
> I love the moon because it's bright.
> I love the stars
> The smell of flowers
> The song that the bird sings.
> I like the robin's red breast
> It is so nice because it's red.
> Thank you God for all these things."

Summer:	A group of children bring forward a ball, a skipping rope, a spade and pail, a yacht and place them on the leader's table.
Prayer:	(Preferably one written by the children.) "Thank you" for all the things we enjoy in the summer.
Bible Reading:	Ps. 74 : 16 and 17 (R.S.V.).
Hymn:	"Thank you" (p. 162)—use also the verses the children have written themselves.
Leader:	A short talk by the leader about the promotion of the oldest Primary children to the Junior department and to new classes. Remind the children that they are all growing up in the Church.
Bible Reading:	Luke 2 : 52.
Prayer:	"We thank you, O God, for our strong, healthy bodies so that we can run and skip and dance and play and enjoy the summer. We praise you that we are growing at home, at school, and in the Church. As we say thank you for the many things we enjoy, help us, O God, to share all these things with others." Amen.
Hymn:	"All things bright and beautiful" (I.P. 1, Tune: Royal Oak) or "God who made the earth" (R.C.H. 20 : 1-4).
Music:	Play the music again.

HELPING OTHERS

Words and Music by
Woodlands Church Primary, Glasgow

1. Mothers cook and Aunties sew
   Father's working all day through
   God's got work for me to do
   And God looks after me.

2. I'll wash the dishes, I'll feed the cat
   I'll make my bed, I'll sweep the mat
   Give me a job and I'll do that
   And God looks after me.

AT CHURCH

In our Church we like to sing,
And we sometimes softly pray,
Thanking God for ev'rything,
God who loves us ev'ry day.

PRAISE TO GOD (78.88.6.)

KENNETH GEORGE FINLAY

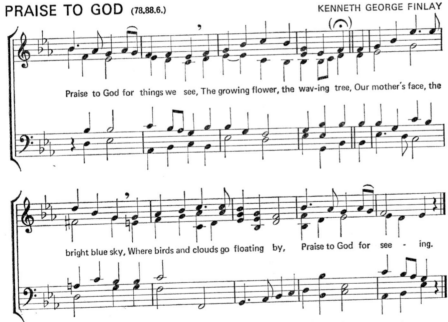

Praise to God for things we see, The growing flower, the wav-ing tree, Our mother's face, the
bright blue sky, Where birds and clouds go floating by, Praise to God for see - ing.

Praise to God for things we hear,
The voices of our playmates dear,
The merry bells, the song of birds,
Stories and tunes and kindly words,
Praise to God for hearing.

Praise to God for things we do,
For fun and games and laughter too.
Our hands to help, our feet to run,
For all our joy, for all our fun.
Praise to God for doing.

HERE WE GO UP TO BETHLEHEM

Tune: Mulberry Bush
Arr.: Aileen Robertson

Here we go up to Bethlehem, Bethlehem, Bethlehem,
Here we go up to Bethlehem
On a cold and frosty morning.

We've got to be taxed in Bethlehem, Bethlehem, Bethlehem,
We've got to be taxed in Bethlehem,
On a cold and frosty morning.

Where shall we stay in Bethlehem, Bethlehem, Bethlehem,
Where shall we stay in Bethlehem,
On a cold and frosty morning.

Sydney Carter.

THE WISE MEN CAME FROM OUT OF THE EAST

Fairy Lullaby
Music Arranged by Aileen Robertson

1. The Wise men came from out of the East,
   From out of the East, from out of the East,
   The Wise men came from out of the East,
   To find the little Lord Jesus.

2. They followed the star to Bethlehem,
   To Bethlehem, to Bethlehem,
   They followed the star to Bethlehem,
   And found the little Lord Jesus.

3. They brought with them their precious gifts,
   Their precious gifts, their precious gifts,
   They brought with them their precious gifts,
   To give to little Lord Jesus.

4. At Christmas children all over the world,
   All over the world, all over the world,
   At Christmas children all over the world,
   Have gifts like little Lord Jesus.

Words of verses 3 and 4 by Mrs. J. Adair

THANK YOU

Arranged by Aileen Robertson

Thank you for waking me this morning
Thank you for giving me today,
Thank you for every new day dawning,
God I'm thanking you.

Thank you for every tree and flower
Thank you for every sky of blue
Thank you I should be every hour,
Truly thanking you.

INFANT HOLY

POLISH NOËL

Infant Holy, Infant lowly,
For His bed a cattle stall;
Oxen lowing, little knowing
Christ the Babe is Lord of all.
Swift are winging Angels singing,
Nowells ringing, Tidings bringing,
Christ the Babe is Lord of all.

CHILDREN, COME!

Chinese Air

1. Jesus said long, long ago,
   "Let the children come to me;"
   They belong to him, you know:
   They are his own family.

2. Children ran to him that day;
   Then he touched them with his hand
   Quietly they heard him pray,
   Every child could understand.

3. That is why our parents come,
   Bringing us from far and near:
   To the Church which is our home—
   House of God, for love is here.

From Music in Christian Education
by Edith Lovell Thomas.
Copyright 1953 by Pierce and Washabaugh.
Used by permission of Abingdon Press.

CHRIST IS RISEN

Tune: "Fernhill"
by Aileen Robertson

"Christ is coming, Christ is coming,
On a donkey, on a donkey,
Hosanna, Hosanna,
We wave our palm branches."

(Written by Lothian Road Church Primary School,
Edinburgh)

"Christ is risen, Christ is risen,
Hallelujah! Hallelujah!
He is with us, He is with us,
Today and for ever."

Cynthia Dean

HAPPY THOUGHT

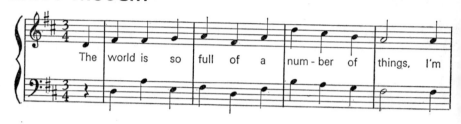

The world is so full of a num-ber of things, I'm

sure we should all be as hap-py as kings.

2. Our friends and our fam'lies,
   Our pets and our play,
   The rain and the sunshine,
   God planned it that way.

3. We thank you, dear God now
   For all these good things:
   We love you, we thank you,
   We're happy as kings

From Songs for the Little Child *by Clara Belle Baker and Caroline Kohlsaat.*
Copyright renewal 1949 by Clara Belle Baker. By permission of Abingdon Press.

GOD, WE THANK YOU
(Tune — Frère Jacques)

Florence Schulz

God, we thank you; God, we thank you For our church,

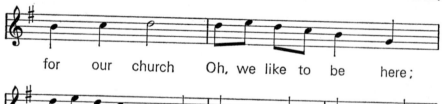

for our church Oh, we like to be here;

Oh, we like to be here Thank you, God; thank you, God.

2. God, we thank you; God, we thank you
   For our church, for our church
   And for all our friends here;
   And for all our friends here
   Thank you, God; thank you, God.

3. God, we thank you; God, we thank you
   For this day, for this day.
   And for all the sunshine;
   And for all the sunshine
   Thank you, God; thank you, God.

From SUMMER WITH NURSERY CHILDREN, by Florence Schulz.
Copyright, United Church Press, Philadelphia, U.S.A. Used by permission.